INTRODUCTION TO THE HISTORICAL BOOKS

INTRODUCTION TO THE HISTORICAL BOOKS

Strategies for Reading

Steven L. McKenzie

WILLIAM B. EERDMANS PUBLISHING COMPANY

GRAND RAPIDS, MICHIGAN / CAMBRIDGE, U.K.

Published 2010 by
Wm. B. Eerdmans Publishing Co.
2140 Oak Industrial Drive N.E., Grand Rapids, Michigan 49505 /
P.O. Box 163, Cambridge CB3 9PU U.K.

Printed in the United States of America

16 15 14 13 12 11 10   7 6 5 4 3 2 1

Library of Congress Cataloging-in-Publication Data

McKenzie, Steven L., 1953-
Introduction to the Historical Books: strategies for reading /
Steven L. McKenzie.
p.   cm.
Includes bibliographical references.
ISBN 978-0-8028-2877-4 (pbk.: alk. paper)
1. Bible. O.T. Historical books — Criticism, interpretation, etc.
2. Bible. O.T. Historical books — Hermeneutics.   I. Title.

BS1205.52.M35   2010
222'.0601 — dc22

2009035865

www.eerdmans.com

Contents

Abbreviations

AASF	Annales Academiae scientiarum fennicae
ABD	*Anchor Bible Dictionary*. Edited by David Noel Freedman. 6 vols. New York: Doubleday, 1992.
Bib	*Biblica*
BWANT	Beiträge zur Wissenschaft von alten und neuen Testament
BZAW	Beihefte zur Zeitschrift für die alttestamentliche Wissenschaft
CBQMS	Catholic Biblical Quarterly Monograph Series
DJD	Discoveries in the Judean Desert
DOTHB	*Dictionary of the Old Testament: Historical Books*. Edited by Bill T. Arnold and H. G. M. Williamson. Downers Grove: InterVarsity, 2005.
Dtr	Deuteronomist, Deuteronomistic
DtrH	Deuteronomistic History
FRLANT	Forschungen zur Religion und Literatur des Alten und Neuen Testaments
GBS	Guides to Biblical Scholarship
HSM	Harvard Semitic Monographs
HTR	*Harvard Theological Review*
HUCA	*Hebrew Union College Annual*
IDBSup	*Interpreter's Dictionary of the Bible: Supplementary Volume*. Edited by Keith Crim. Nashville: Abingdon, 1976.
JPS	Jewish Publication Society
JSOT	*Journal for the Study of the Old Testament*

JSOTSup	Journal for the Study of the Old Testament: Supplement Series
JTS	*Journal of Theological Studies*
LXX	Septuagint
MT	Masoretic Text
NAB	New American Bible
NIDB	*New Interpreter's Dictionary of the Bible.* Ed. Katherine Doob Sakenfeld. 5 vols. Nashville: Abingdon, 2006-9.
NOAB	*The New Oxford Annotated Bible.* 3rd ed. New York: Oxford University Press, 2001.
NRSV	New Revised Standard Version
OBO	Orbis biblicus et orientalis
OG	Old Greek
OTG	Old Testament Guides
OTL	The Old Testament Library
OtSt	Oudtestamentische Studiën
SBLMS	Society of Biblical Literature Monograph Series
SBT	Studies in Biblical Theology
SDSSRL	Studies in the Dead Sea Scrolls and Related Literature
VT	*Vetus Testamentum*
VTSup	Supplements to Vetus Testamentum
WBC	Word Biblical Commentary
ZAW	*Zeitschrift für die alttestamentliche Wissenschaft*

1

In Search of the Historical Books

Canons and Communities

The term "Historical Books" in reference to a portion or portions of the Bible is unfortunate. It is unfortunate, first of all, because it is difficult to determine which books fall into this category and why. In fact, different books are placed in this category by different faith communities and by different scholars with roots in the different faith communities. The designation Historical Books is a distinctly Christian one, appearing first in the writings of Christian leaders of the fourth century c.e. There is a good chance that Jewish readers will not even find the category of Historical Books in their Bibles. Instead, the books of Joshua, Judges, 1-2 Samuel, and 1-2 Kings are grouped among the Prophets, in the Jewish canon, possibly as a subunit entitled Former Prophets. Other books sometimes included in this category — Ruth, Esther, Ezra-Nehemiah, and 1-2 Chronicles (usually in that order) — are all found in the third major section of the Hebrew Bible, the Writings.[1]

Among Christians, Protestants can open their Bibles and find a canonical unit of the Old Testament under the heading Historical Books that encompasses the works of Joshua, Judges, Ruth, 1-2 Samuel, 1-2 Kings,

---

1. Thus, *The Jewish Study Bible* edition of the JPS Tanakh translation (Oxford: Oxford University Press, 2004) vi, under the headings Nevi'im and Ketuvim, Hebrew for "Prophets" and "Writings," respectively.

1-2 Chronicles, Ezra-Nehemiah, and Esther.[2] Roman Catholic readers can find the same heading with the same entries but supplemented with Tobit, Judith, and 1-2 Maccabees.[3] Protestants do not consider the latter books to be Scripture, but relegate them to the Apocrypha. Greek Orthodox Christians' Bibles include not only Tobit, Judith, and 1-2 Maccabees in this category but 1 Esdras and 3 Maccabees as well.[4]

Scholarly treatments of the Historical Books add a further variation. While some follow one of the canonical divisions noted above, usually reflecting the religious stance or background of the author or publication,[5] others bracket Ruth and Esther from consideration as well as the Apocryphal/Deuterocanonical books, though not always with explanations of their reasons for so doing.[6]

The present volume follows this latter scholarly convention by treating the books of Joshua, Judges, 1-2 Samuel, 1-2 Kings, 1-2 Chronicles, and Ezra-Nehemiah. This choice is based partly on canon. My focus is materials within the Hebrew Bible, which does not include Tobit, Judith, 1 Esdras,

2. So, e.g., the NOAB, p. vii. Curiously, though, the NOAB lists "The Historical Books," along with "The Poetical and Wisdom Books," as subcategories of "The Hebrew Bible."

3. Cf. the *Saint Mary's Press College Study Bible* edition of the NAB (Winona, MN: St. Mary's, 2006) vi. The curious listing of the books of Genesis–Ruth under "Pentateuch" with "The Historical Books" including 1 Samuel–2 Maccabees in the 1971 edition of the NAB published by Nelson was the result of a printer's error, according to Mary Sperry of the U.S. Conference of Catholic Bishops as communicated to me on 19 March 2008 by Bishop Richard J. Sklba of the Archdiocese of Milwaukee. I am grateful to Bishop Sklba for his assistance with my query.

4. See the *Orthodox Study Bible* (Nashville: Nelson, 2008), esp. XIII. The Old Testament portion of this Bible is a translation of the Greek Septuagint (LXX).

5. So Robert B. Chisholm, Jr., *Interpreting the Historical Books: An Exegetical Handbook.* Handbooks for Old Testament Exegesis (Grand Rapids: Kregel, 2006), and Victor P. Hamilton, *Handbook on the Historical Books* (Grand Rapids: Baker, 2001), both Evangelical Christians, follow the Protestant canon and include Ruth and Esther among the books they discuss.

6. Richard D. Nelson, *The Historical Books.* Interpreting Biblical Texts (Nashville: Abingdon, 1998) 17, indicates that Ruth and Esther, as well as apocryphal books like Judith, 1–2 Maccabees, and presumably Tobit, though arguably historical books, are not covered in his volume. The *Dictionary of the Old Testament: Historical Books,* ed. Bill T. Arnold and H. G. M. Williamson (Downers Grove: InterVarsity, 2005), contains no entries for Esther, Ruth, or the Apocryphal/Deuterocanonical books and no explanation within the volume for their exclusion. Its accompanying dust jacket notes only that it presents articles on historical topics and "major articles focused on the books of Joshua, Judges, Samuel, Kings, Chronicles, Ezra and Nehemiah."

or 1-4 Maccabees, and which indicates that Ruth and Esther were completely distinct from the Former Prophets and from Chronicles-Ezra-Nehemiah.

The choice is also based partly on genre. None of the books treated here — or any other books in the Bible, for that matter — refer to themselves or their content as "history." That would be virtually impossible, since the word "history" is Greek in origin. (In the next chapter we will explore in detail both the significance and definition of the literary genre of history writing in the Bible.) But the books of Joshua–Kings as a canonical unit have long been recognized as comprising, either at the authorial or the editorial level, a running history of Israel. Similarly, the works of Chronicles and Ezra-Nehemiah are another such history, again at least editorially. Ruth and Esther, in contrast, are examples of short stories or *novellas* rather than of history writing. At most, one might refer to Ruth and Esther as historiography rather than history writing (see below on the distinction).

It should be noted that one might legitimately include the books of the Torah or Pentateuch — Genesis, Exodus, Leviticus, Numbers, and Deuteronomy — within the genre of history writing and in the category of "Historical Books." Here, however, pragmatic considerations influence my decision (and that of the publisher) not to include them. As is typical of series such as this, the Pentateuchal books are dealt with in another volume.

The Significance of Genre

"Genre," a term borrowed from French, means "type" and is used to refer to categories of literature, as well as music, film, and the like. Literature has many different genres and subgenres. Broadly, we think of two major genres: fiction and nonfiction. But then there are different genres within each of those two categories: e.g., novel and romance as examples of fiction; biography and poetry as instances of nonfiction. Genres are fluid rather than fixed, so that one work can incorporate many genres. Thus, a textbook (nonfiction) might incorporate several short stories (fiction). A novel could contain poems or other nonfictional pieces. Alice Walker's *The Color Purple*, for instance, is a novel (fiction) that includes letters (a nonfiction category), which are, nonetheless, fictional.

Mutual recognition of genre, including the changing of genres and variations within a genre, are an integral part of the communication process between authors and readers. Proper recognition of genre is crucial for understanding a literary work. All readers make assumptions about genre as they approach a literary work. These assumptions, in turn, lead to expectations. Mistaken assumptions and expectations cause confusion and misunderstanding. Imagine, for instance, the confusion of someone who reads science fiction as history (as is the premise of the movie *Galaxy Quest*) or the even more disastrous consequences that would ensue if a surgeon were to construe the instruction manual for a new surgical instrument as fiction.

Such a disastrous scenario is unlikely to take place precisely because authors and readers usually share the same culture. Recognizing genre is largely a function of culture. Like learning a language, it is something that a person absorbs or learns subconsciously while growing up in a particular culture. Literary works rarely identify their genre. Rather, a person learns "automatically" to recognize the genre of a given literary work produced within his/her own culture simply by virtue of having grown up in that culture, without really thinking about it or necessarily being able to explain how or why the recognition took place.

It can be much harder for people outside of a culture to recognize that culture's literary genres. However, just as a language has grammatical rules, so there are guidelines and clues for discerning genre. Such clues sometimes come in the different physical forms of literary works. We can easily distinguish newspapers, magazines, and books from one another, even if they are in an unfamiliar language. In antiquity, letters, inscriptions, royal decrees, and other documents were also presented in different physical forms. But these physical differences disappeared in the process of the Bible's formation, and readers now have to rely on clues within the text to determine genre.

The clues about genre typically come in the form of specific features within a text — often at its beginning or end — that signal its genre and lead the reader to adopt a set of assumptions and expectations about the text's content. Consider the following phrases: "Dateline Tokyo," "Dear Sir/Madam," and "Once upon a time." In these three simple phrases the beginnings of three different genres of literature are easily recognizable: a newspaper article, a business letter, and a fairy tale, respectively. We would recognize them quite apart from their physical form, for instance, if they were sent electronically. Each raises a set of expectations within us as readers. For "Dateline Tokyo" we expect to read a report about recent events in Japan, not a fairy tale. For "Dear Sir/Madam" we expect the document to end with "Sincerely" rather than "They lived happily ever after."

However, literature is an art form, and creative writers can vary and mix genres, playing with readers' expectations, for creative ends. The use of a nonfictional genre for fictional ends in *The Color Purple* is one example. But on a more mundane level, imagine parents who want to make a point about not having heard from their son, who is away at college. They might write a personal letter in the guise of a business letter, beginning "Dear Sir" and ending "Sincerely." The young man's girlfriend in the same situation might make a not-too-subtle point about their relationship by composing a fairy tale beginning "Once upon a time" but without the typical "They lived happily ever after." Thus, an author can convey a message simply through the creative use of genre.

Genre and the Bible

As an integral element in the process of communication, properly discerning the genres in the Bible is just as crucial to understanding it as comprehending the languages in which it was written and its cultural and historical background. Yet, serious consideration of genre is often neglected when it comes to the Bible. As a result, modern readers frequently approach portions of the Bible with an incorrect set of assumptions and expectations. This typically occurs in two respects — readers either incorrectly identify the genre of the biblical work or text they are reading or, more commonly, they assume that the ancient Israelite genre is the same as the modern Western one.

The book of Jonah is a good illustration of the first problem. Like the books of Ruth and Esther, Jonah is a short story that is often misconstrued as history. But unlike Ruth and Esther, Jonah is best characterized as satire or parody. This is apparent upon close reading from a number of features in the book, including its ubiquitous use of hyperbole and the overall ludicrous nature of the story:[7] Jonah, the prophet, is the only character in the

7. For a detailed discussion, see my *How to Read the Bible: History, Prophecy, Literature — Why Modern Readers Need to Know the Difference and What It Means for Faith Today* (New York: Oxford University Press, 2005) 1-13.

book who disobeys God. He tries to run away, despite his confession that Yahweh is the maker of sea and dry land. His reason for fleeing is fear of his potential success, for he does not want the people of Nineveh to repent and save themselves from destruction. And succeed he does, more than any other prophet in the Bible. After being returned to his mission in the belly of a divinely-appointed fish, Jonah's curt, one-sentence threat (presumably in Hebrew) induces all one hundred thousand people of Nineveh (who do not speak Hebrew) — along with their animals! — to change their wicked ways. Instead of being pleased at this success, as one would expect a prophet to be, Jonah is upset. A divinely-provided object lesson reveals that he cares more about a plant than he does about the myriad of inhabitants in Nineveh.

As with most biblical literature, there is nothing in Jonah that explicitly identifies its genre. Hence, every reader makes an assumption about its genre, and the decision to read it as history is every bit as much an assumption as the decision to read it as satire. Moreover, the features described above — exaggeration, portrait of Jonah as a ridiculous figure, and the like — are strong indications that the book was intended as something other than straightforward reporting of the past. Its intent seems to be to teach a lesson against prejudice and the hatred of non-Israelites by ridiculing Jonah (whose name means "dove," a possible symbol of Israel) as a negative example of just such attitudes. Interpreting the book as history is like reading science fiction or fantasy as history and actually undermines its richness, creativity, and purpose!

History and History Writing

The second incorrect assumption — assuming that an ancient genre is identical to a modern one — is more complicated. This is another reason that the designation "Historical Books" is unfortunate. It tends to arouse false expectations on the part of readers, especially modern Western readers, about the nature of the literature. History, for most modern Westerners, is what happened in the past, pure and simple, and writing history means recounting exactly what happened in the past. The discipline of history is viewed as a kind of journalism and the historian as a courtroom witness, who is under oath to tell "the truth, the whole truth, and nothing but the truth" about the past — or at least that is the objective. Most people, especially these days, would probably admit that historians, like journalists, may be biased. After all, no one is completely objective. If they thought about it, most people would also likely recognize that writing history involves interpretation and that it is impossible to know every detail about what happened in the past. Further reflection might lead to the conclusion that all history is in fact interpretation, at least in some sense, since it is impossible to know or completely understand any event of the past in all its details and with all its complex causes. Still, we do not generally contemplate these things when looking for information about a particular event or episode of the past. History remains for us the "facts of the past," and history writing is the reporting of those facts.

This is all the more true when it comes to the Bible's account of history. It is, after all, the *Bible* — sacred literature, holy Scripture, the inspired word of God. Surely God knows all history, so the Bible's "Historical Books" should be historically accurate. Only, that does not appear to be the case — at least not according to the leading biblical and archaeological scholarship. Most biblical scholars and archaeologists believe that major events recounted in the Bible, such as the flood, the exodus from Egypt, and the conquest of Canaan either never occurred or did not happen in the way the Bible describes them.

When Bible scholars and archaeologists come to conclusions like these, the typical first reaction, particularly among people of faith, is to dismiss them as biased. In more conservative circles, the charge is sometimes echoed that such scholars are godless disbelievers who look down on any form of faith and are driven to "convert" others to their atheistic nihilism. But this stereotype rings true in very few instances. Most Bible scholars and archaeologists come from faith traditions, and many, if not most, retain their traditions in some form. If they abandon faith or move into a different stream of tradition over the matter of the Bible's historical reliability, it may be because they or their initial tradition had too narrow an understanding of history.

Biblical scholarship in one sense has been around for two thousand years or more — ever since the Bible was written. However, as an academic discipline, biblical scholarship is a product of the Enlightenment and began three hundred or so years ago. Scholarship of this sort is "critical" — not in the sense of being negatively oriented toward the Bible, but in the sense of being "careful," paying attention to details and problems in the biblical text and seeking solutions for them. Biblical scholarship also makes use of comparative history and literature from cognate cultures and of the findings of archaeology. In the past fifty years or so, archaeology has become especially scientific in orientation and has raised serious doubts about the historical validity of some of the leading events narrated in the Bible.

Rather than denying the results of historical research or dismissing its practitioners as wrongly motivated, it is appropriate to ask whether the genre of the Bible's "Historical Books" has been properly understood. In other words, the source of the discrepancy may lie not with the Bible per se but with the way in which it has been read. A better understanding of biblical history writing in its ancient context may help to resolve the tensions between the Bible's account and historical analyses.

The question of the nature of history writing in the Bible has been raised more acutely in recent decades as the number and nature of historical discrepancies have increased. In the first half of the twentieth century, two renowned German scholars, Gerhard von Rad and Martin Noth, made inroads in this direction. Von Rad argued that the "Court History" in 2 Samuel 13–1 Kings 2 represented the "beginnings of historical writing in Israel" because of its "secular" attribution of events to human rather than divine causation.[8] Both Noth and von Rad considered the Bible's history, though based on some actual historical events, as primarily a collection of traditions and stories about the past. Both used the ambiguous German term *Geschichte* ("story") rather than *Historie* to refer to this history. Von Rad, in particular, referred to it as *Heilsgeschichte,* "salvation history," that is, the story about Israel's beliefs upon which its religious practices were founded.

But it was John Van Seters in 1983 who first tried to define history writing in the Bible as a literary genre in the context of comparable materials in other parts of the ancient world, notably Greece, Mesopotamia, the Hittites, and Egypt.[9] Van Seters's study called into question the common assumption that ancient historians, including the biblical writers, had the same definition of history and history writing as we do. On the contrary, he sought to show that these writers understood their task to be something

---

8. Gerhard von Rad, "The Beginnings of Historical Writing in Ancient Israel," in *The Problem of the Hexateuch and Other Essays* (New York: McGraw-Hill, 1966) 166-204.

9. John Van Seters, *In Search of History: Historiography in the Ancient World and the Origins of Biblical History* (New Haven: Yale University Press, 1983).

quite different than simply relating what happened in the past. Because they have had a significant impact on biblical scholarship, Van Seters's ideas merit detailed characterization.

Van Seters began with the definition of history formulated by the Dutch historian Johan Huizinga: "History is the intellectual form in which a civilization renders account to itself of its past."[10] This definition has three key elements, and Van Seters explored each of them for the understanding of the Bible's historical literature.

History. On the basis of Huizinga's definition, Van Seters distinguished between *history writing* as the genre in which a civilization or nation tried to render an account of its collective past and *historiography* as a more general term for all historical texts, such as annals, king lists, battle accounts, and so on. Historiographical materials preserved in Egypt, Mesopotamia, and by the Hittites have long been recognized. However, Van Seters contended that true history writing developed first in Israel and then in Greece, which he argued produced the closest analogs, especially in the work of Herodotus, the so-called father of history.

Intellectual form. Van Seters discerned two facets in particular of Herodotus's work that constituted it as an intellectual form. First, Herodotus engaged in personal research and investigation. He gathered first-hand information, especially about geography and social customs, as well as traditions, legends, and even myths of local peoples about whom he wrote. All of these kinds of materials were an integral part of Herodotus's history. In fact, the basic meaning of the Greek term *historiē*, from which our word "history" is derived, is "investigations" or "researches."

The second facet of Herodotus's work that Van Seters emphasized as constituting an intellectual form was that he made a written record of the traditions he received. It was Herodotus's crafting of his sources, both oral and written, into a written, unified whole that set his work apart from that of the ancient Greek storytellers (or "logographers") who preceded him. Thus, ancient history writing was not the result of the gradual accumulation of traditions, as has sometimes been assumed. Rather, it was the deliberate product of a literate society, and literary creativity played an important role in its composition.

---

10. "A Definition of the Concept of History," in *Philosophy and History: Essays Presented to Ernst Cassirer,* ed. Raymond Klibansky and H. J. Paton (1936; repr. New York: Harper & Row, 1963) 9.

Several features of ancient Greek history writing illustrate the freedom and literary creativity exercised by its authors, and these features are often shared by the Bible's historical literature. For one thing, there is the question of structure. Ancient historians used a variety of structuring techniques. One of the most common of these, particularly in Herodotus, was the simple stringing together of different stories and episodes, often with their own introductions and conclusions, but with little or no verbal connection between them. This technique is called "parataxis."

Another such technique was the use of genealogies as framing or structuring devices. The book of Genesis in the Bible does this, and 1-2 Chronicles begins with nine chapters of genealogies. Ancient Greek historians also used speeches and narrative formulas for structuring purposes. Such speeches were typically invented by the historians, in both wording and substance, according to what was deemed appropriate to the occasion.[11] After all, the historians were usually not present at the occasions when speeches were delivered, especially those in the distant past. We will witness the use of this technique in the Bible as well, in both the Former Prophets and Chronicles. In addition to speeches, sometimes these historians even invented stories and source citations in order to fill in gaps in their work or link materials together. Again, this technique also seems to be present in the Bible.

A civilization renders account to itself of its past. For Huizinga and for Van Seters, ancient history writing presupposed not only a literate society but a corporate one as well. History writing expressed the corporate identity of a nation or civilization — how it envisioned itself — its make-up and the principles and ideals it represented or embodied. Once the corporate identity behind history writing is understood, the purpose of the genre becomes clearer. This purpose was not primarily to relate past events exactly as they happened. Rather, the primary purpose of ancient history writing was to explain the present by "rendering an account" of the past. In Greece, and Van Seters would argue in Israel too, this "rendering an account" entailed assessing responsibility for and passing judgment on a nation's past actions as having consequences and implications for the author's present. This means that ancient historians had axes to grind — theological or political points to make. Put another way, the an-

---

11. A point emphasized by the eminent classicist Moses I. Finley, in *Ancient History: Evidence and Models* (New York: Viking, 1986) 13.

cient historians' primary concern was not detailing exactly what happened in the past as much as it was showing how the "causes" of the past brought about the "effects" of the present, in other words, interpreting the meaning of the past for the present.

The cause-effect explanations employed by ancient history writers were not scientific in nature as they might be today but typically had to do with moral and religious matters. Greek historians, for instance, used what we would classify as myth or legend as causes of the past leading to the present. This was partly out of necessity. Myths and legends were the only sources available for the distant past, which had not produced written records. Even history writers who did not believe the myths were compelled to use them because they had no other sources. These writers often "rationalized" the myths they incorporated by offering more "scientific" interpretation for them. The main point, however, is that, as a whole, ancient history writing was in many ways closer to storytelling about the past and moralizing on the basis of it than it was to the journalistic reporting of facts.

Applying his observations from Huizinga's definition and from Greek history writing to the Bible, Van Seters proposed five defining criteria for identifying history writing in ancient Israel:[12]

1. a specific form of tradition in its own right rather than the accidental accumulation of traditional material;
2. considers the reason for recalling the past and the significance of past events and not primarily the accurate reporting of the past;
3. examines the (primarily moral) causes in the past of present conditions and circumstances;
4. national or corporate in nature; and
5. literary and an important part of a people's corporate tradition.

The Bible's History Writing as Etiology and Theology

The "Historical Books" of the Bible exemplify the criteria laid out by Van Seters for the genre of ancient history. First, the biblical authors conducted *research* into traditional materials and collected stories and traditions (cri-

---

12. *In Search of History,* 4-5.

terion 1). This is illustrated on the surface by the citation of various traditional sources that the biblical writers claim to have consulted. However, these sources do not appear, by and large, to have been quoted verbatim. Rather, the biblical authors adapted and fashioned them into literary products whose interests were national in scope (criteria 4 and 5).

Criteria 2 and 3 are particularly significant for the Bible's "Historical Books," whose *etiological* nature has long been noted by scholars. The word "etiology" (also spelled "aetiology") is derived from the Greek word *aitia,* meaning "cause." An etiology is a story that explains the *cause* or origin of a given phenomenon — a cultural practice or social custom, a biological circumstance, even a geological formation. It is not a scientific explanation and is not historical in the modern sense of an event that actually took place in the past. Instead, it is a story that "renders an account," that is, offers some explanation, of present conditions and circumstances based on past causes. Etiologies, in fact, can be very imaginative.

The Bible's "Historical Books" are etiological in the sense that they seek to "render an account" of the past — to provide an explanation for circumstances or conditions in the historian's day. Whether the events they relate as past causes or explanations actually took place is of secondary importance. This is not to say that all of the traditions recorded as part of Israel's history writing are fictional. Many, perhaps even most, are no doubt based on actual events of the past. But a proper understanding of ancient history writing allows for the incorporation of nonhistorical and even fictional narratives. To attempt to read the account of Israel's history in the Bible strictly as a record of actual events is to misconstrue its genre and to force it to do something it was not intended to do. This is because the main concern of the Bible's "Historical Books" is not to describe exactly what happened in the past but to provide explanations from the past for Israel's self-understanding. Key to that self-understanding is Israel's perception of its relationship to its God, Yahweh, in whom ancient Israelite historians found the ultimate explanation for their people's origin and present state. Thus, in the Bible, as in ancient Greek literature, history was written for an ideological purpose. History writing was theology.

2

The Works behind the Historical Books

The individual Historical Books are actually constituent parts of two larger works, which are, in turn, closely related to one another. Scholars are essentially in agreement on this point. They disagree, however, about when and how these larger works were constituted. Specifically, were the works written as wholes and subsequently divided into individual books, or were the books written as distinct units and later combined editorially into larger works? The answer to this question is probably different for each of the two large works.

The Deuteronomistic History

The books of Joshua, Judges, 1-2 Samuel, and 1-2 Kings (i.e., the Former Prophets in the Hebrew canon) comprise a lengthy, running story as the following overview of their contents shows.

Joshua	Conquest of the land of Canaan under the leadership of Joshua, Moses' successor (chs. 1–12), and the division of the land among the tribes of Israel (chs. 13–24)
Judges	Stories of military deliverers who rescue Israel from military oppressors at a time "when there was no king in Israel"
1 Samuel	Samuel the prophet designated to anoint Israel's first king, Saul, who is subsequently rejected in favor of David

2 Samuel   David's reign as king, first of Judah, then of Israel
1 Kings   Solomon's reign (chs. 1–11) and the history of Israel and
             Judah from the division through the reign of Ahab
2 Kings   Continued history of Israel and Judah until their respective
             destructions

Until 1943, scholars tended to view these books either as an extension of the Pentateuch or as originally individual compositions strung together in a final edition. As an extension of the Pentateuch there were two basic models. One envisioned a "*Hexa*teuch" or original work in *six* books instead of five (*Penta*teuch), that is, encompassing the first six books of the Bible, Genesis through Joshua. The other considered the *nine* books of Genesis through Kings (counting 1-2 Samuel and 1-2 Kings as one book each and not counting Ruth, whose placement is different in the Hebrew Bible than in English Bibles) as an original unit; scholars adopted the name "*Ennea*teuch" for this theory. This numbers game changed radically in 1943 when Martin Noth, one of the giants in the field of Biblical Studies, separated the Pentateuch, or most of it, and proposed instead that the books of the Former Prophets, along with the book of Deuteronomy at their head, were originally written as a unit — a single, extended history of Israel that he called the Deuteronomistic History (DtrH for short).[1]

Noth believed that the author of the DtrH was an individual living in the Babylonian exile (which began in 586 B.C.E.). Specifically, Noth dated the DtrH to 562, or shortly thereafter, because that was the date of the last event it records (2 Kgs 25:27-30). The Deuteronomistic Historian or Deuteronomist (abbreviated Dtr) probably lived in Mizpah, the administrative capital of Judah following the destruction of Jerusalem, and thus had access to oral and written traditions about Israel and Judah. Those traditions were the sources for his History. Dtr selected from among the traditions he collected and forged them into a unified whole through various techniques of linking and harmonization. He was, therefore, both an editor and an author. He revised and reworked older traditions and stories but also composed materials on occasion, especially speeches attributed to

---

1. Martin Noth, *Überlieferungsgeschichtliche Studien*, vol. 1: *Die sammelnden und bearbeitenden Geschichtswerke im Alten Testament*, 3rd ed. (Tübingen: Niemeyer, 1967). The first part of the book is available in English as *The Deuteronomistic History*. JSOTSup 15, 2nd ed. (Sheffield: JSOT, 1991).

leading characters (Joshua 23; 1 Samuel 12; 1 Kgs 8:12-53) and summative reflections (Judg 2:11-23; 2 Kings 17). That such passages emanated from the same hand was clear from the fact that they shared a common writing style and vocabulary as well as a common theological outlook. Noth also argued that the books of the DtrH shared a common chronology, although it had become obscured in transmission.

Noth believed that the purpose of the DtrH was etiological, "etiology" referring to a story that explains the origin of something. In this case, the etiology actually explained an ending, the ending of Israel and Judah as nations. Noth referred to the DtrH as *eine Ätiologie des Nuls,* which might best be translated "an etiology of destruction." Its purpose, he thought, was to explain how the ultimate demise of Israel and Judah had come about as a direct result of habitual sin just as Deuteronomy had forecast in the warnings voiced by Moses. Dtr had inherited an early form of the book of Deuteronomy as one of the most important of his sources. He placed it at the head of his History as articulating the standard by which Israel would be judged. Dtr also adopted Deuteronomy's doctrine that prosperity and disaster were the inevitable results of righteousness and sin, respectively, and presented his history of Israel as the working out of this doctrine, at least the negative side of it. It was this dependence on Deuteronomy that led Noth to adopt the name Deuteronomistic History.

The response to Noth's proposal over the past several decades has unfolded in three stages. During the first twenty-five years or so following the appearance of Noth's book, scholars were generally persuaded by his idea that Deuteronomy plus the Former Prophets was an original unit. One of the reasons for this immediate positive reception was the fact, long recognized by scholars, that Deuteronomy was distinct from the first four books of the Pentateuch and seemed to have more in common with books that follow it than with those that precede it. Noth's proposal just appeared intuitively to be correct.

However, Gerhard von Rad, a figure whose scholarly repute equaled Noth's, questioned the suggestion that Dtr's purpose was negative.[2] Von Rad focused on the promise to David in 2 Samuel 7 and argued that it

---

2. Gerhard von Rad, "Die deuteronomistische Geschichtstheologie in den Königs-büchern," *Deuteronomium-Studien,* B, 52-64. FRLANT n.s. 40 (Göttingen: Vandenhoeck & Ruprecht, 1947) = "The Deuteronomistic Theology of History in the Books of Kings," *Studies in Deuteronomy,* 74-91. SBT 9 (Chicago: Regnery, 1953).

functioned in the DtrH to explain the postponement of God's judgment against Judah. Then, the final reference to Jehoiachin's release from prison in 2 Kgs 25:27-30 expressed a muted hope about where God could begin to restore his people. Similarly, Hans Walter Wolff expressed doubt that an Israelite writer would go to such great length and detail as that found in the DtrH merely to show that Israel and Judah "got what they deserved." Wolff found a thread of hope in the recurring theme of repentance in the DtrH.[3]

A second stage in the history of response to the theory of the DtrH began in the late 1960s and 1970s with the alternative proposals by Rudolf Smend of the University of Göttingen in Germany and Frank Cross of Harvard. Noth had found plenty of secondary additions to Dtr's work but had denied any systematic redaction or later editing of it. Smend and Cross argued for just such redactional or editorial activity.

In a 1971 article Smend focused on the books of Joshua and Judges.[4] In addition to the basic layer of Dtr writing or editing, Smend found a second layer which, he believed, reflected a special interest in law. He adopted the siglum DtrN (for Nomistic) for this second layer, in contrast to Noth's original Dtr layer, which Smend designated DtrG (for *Grundschrift,* meaning "basic writing").

More important than Smend's article was the development of his ideas by his students, especially Walter Dietrich and Timo Veijola. Dietrich argued for a third, Prophetic redactional layer (DtrP) between DtrG and DtrN in 1-2 Kings that was, in fact, responsible for the book's basic structure as well as most of its stories about prophets.[5] Veijola took this same approach in two sequential studies on Samuel.[6] This "layer model" of the

---

3. Hans Walter Wolff, "Das Kerygma des deuteronomistischen Geschichtswerk," *ZAW* 73 (1961) 171-86 = "The Kerygma of the Deuteronomic Historical Work," in *The Vitality of Old Testament Traditions,* ed. Walter Brueggemann and Wolff, 83-100, 2nd ed. (Atlanta: John Knox, 1982).

4. Rudolf Smend, "Das Gesetz und die Völker: Ein Beitrag zur deuteronomistischen Redaktionsgeschichte," in *Probleme biblischer Theologie: Gerhard von Rad zum 70. Geburtstag,* ed. Hans Walter Wolff, 494-509 (Munich: Kaiser, 1971).

5. Walter Dietrich, *Prophetie und Geschichte: Eine redaktionsgeschichtliche Untersuchung zum deuteronomistischen Geschichtswerk.* FRLANT 108 (Göttingen: Vandenhoeck & Ruprecht, 1972).

6. Timo Veijola, *Das ewige Dynastie: David und die Entstehung seiner Dynastie nach der deuteronomistischen Darstellung.* AASF B 193 (Helsinki: Suomalainen Tiedeakatemia, 1975); and *Das Königtum in der Beurteilung der deuteronomistischen Historiographie.* AASF B 198 (Helsinki: Suomalainen Tiedeakatemia, 1977).

so-called Smend or Göttingen school has become dominant in Europe. It has also become increasingly complex, as adherents have proposed additional Dtr redactors in different books as well as distinct hands within a given Dtr layer or "school" (e.g., DtrN[1], DtrN[2], DtrN[3]). The compositional model that lies behind this proliferation of redactors seems to be drawn from later Talmudic literature, which records the opinions of different rabbis about the interpretation of scriptural texts.

In contrast to the layer model of Smend, the redactional proposal of the so-called Cross or Harvard school conceives of the DtrH as having been composed in blocks of material. Its beginning point was an article by Cross that accepted certain pre-Noth arguments for a preexilic edition of the book of Kings, such as the use of the expression "to this day" in texts that presuppose the existence of the kingdom of Judah (e.g., 2 Kgs 8:22).[7] Cross further noted two contrasting themes that run throughout 1-2 Kings: the "sin of Jeroboam," which climaxes with the fall of Samaria (2 Kings 17), and the faithfulness of David, which reaches its climax with the reforming king Josiah (2 Kings 22-23). Based on these two themes, Cross suggested that the DtrH was originally written in the seventh century b.c.e. as a propaganda work supporting Josiah's reform movement. Cross called this initial edition Dtr[1] and suggested that it had been revised by a second, exilic editor (Dtr[2]) who added the current ending (2 Kgs 23:25b–25:30) as well as a series of glosses that presupposed the exile in some way. Cross's basic idea has proven particularly influential in North America, where it has been refined and promulgated by his students.[8] Some proponents have argued for more extensive Dtr[2] influence or posited pre-Dtr[1] editions, such as a collection of northern prophetic stories or an even earlier Dtr edition in the reign of King Hezekiah (715-687 b.c.e.).

While there were, to be sure, scholars who continued to subscribe to Noth's theory of the DtrH as the product of a single, exilic Dtr, it is safe to say that many, if not most scholars from the 1970s through the 1990s

---

7. Frank Moore Cross, Jr., "The Structure of the Deuteronomic History," *Perspectives in Jewish Learning.* Annual of the College of Jewish Studies 3 (Chicago: Spertus College of Judaica, 1968) 9-24. Published in revised form in Cross, *Canaanite Myth and Hebrew Epic: Essays in the History of the Religion of Israel* (Cambridge, MA: Harvard University Press, 1973) 274-89.

8. Cf. esp. Richard D. Nelson, *The Double Redaction of the Deuteronomistic History.* JSOTSup 18 (Sheffield: JSOT, 1981). Although not a student of Cross's, Nelson wrote this book, originally his doctoral dissertation, under Patrick Miller, who was Cross's student.

adopted one of the two redactional models. This led to the third stage in the study of the DtrH since Noth, which is best characterized as the dissipation of consensus. Beginning in the late 1990s and to the present day, an increasing variety of opinions about the origin and nature of the Former Prophets has been voiced. In addition to those who hold to Noth's initial theory and those who accept Smend's or Cross's redactional variations on this theory, more and more scholars, especially in Europe, are expressing doubt about the very existence of the DtrH as an original unit. In many ways, this is a full-circle return to pre-Noth scholarship, with some scholars advocating anew the idea of a Hexateuch and others preferring to see the Former Prophets as independent books that were first united under a thin, Deuteronomistic veneer at a very late date. So far, this position is primarily a critique of the tradition following Noth rather than a comprehensive alternative, and no compelling reconstruction has yet emerged from the chaos of viewpoints to replace the DtrH model.[9] As a result, the theory of an original DtrH remains dominant at present, though there is widespread disagreement about the specifics of its authorship, date, and purpose.

In this book, I continue to assume the existence of the DtrH more or less in the guise attributed to it by Noth. That is, while fully acknowledging the use of older sources and the presence of later additions, Noth's explanation that Deuteronomy + the Former Prophets is an original unit by a single, exilic author still seems to me the most economical. Noth's understanding of Dtr's purpose in writing, moreover, has been reinforced and improved by Van Seters's exploration of history writing as an ancient genre, as discussed in the previous chapter. Dtr was a true ancient historian in that he sought to offer a comprehensive, written explanation of Israel's national past that had brought about its present situation. In the treatment of individual books in the DtrH, we will explore how Dtr shaped his source material to effect this purpose.

---

9. A new study by Thomas Römer, *The So-Called Deuteronomistic History: A Sociological, Historical, and Literary Introduction* (London: T&T Clark, 2005), is not exactly an alternative, since it retains the DtrH, but presents an ingenious combination of the different proposals into a comprehensive, if complex, synthesis. In his view, the DtrH began as a loose collection of different genres underlying portions of Deuteronomy, Joshua, Samuel, and Kings, written by elites as propaganda supporting administrative, political, and religious centralization under Josiah. The collection first became the DtrH under the impulse of the crisis of the Babylonian exile and received further editing in the Persian period. It then disappeared as a unit with the incorporation of Deuteronomy into the Torah.

18

The "Chronicler's History"

The Bible contains a second historical corpus that covers much the same period and material as the DtrH. The overlap may be illustrated as follows:

DtrH	Chronicler's History
Moses reviews the law in the wilderness (Deuteronomy)	—
Conquest of Canaan (Joshua)	—
Period of the Judges (Judges)	—
Samuel and Saul (1 Samuel)	—
Reign of David (2 Samuel)	Reign of David (1 Chronicles)
Kingdoms of Israel and Judah (1-2 Kings)	Kingdom of Judah (2 Chronicles)
—	Return from exile and rebuilding of temple (Ezra-Nehemiah)

The table is somewhat misleading, since 1 Chronicles in a sense covers history before David through its genealogies in chs. 1–9. Also, 2 Chronicles occasionally deals with Israel, but primarily when its history overlaps with Judah's.

Like the term "Historical Books," the title "Chronicler's History" is misleading and not entirely appropriate. This is so for three reasons. First, readers may confuse the book of Chronicles with the "Chronicles of the Kings of Israel and Judah" referred to in the book of Kings. Since Chronicles was almost certainly written later and used Kings as one of its principal sources, it was not the source cited in Kings. Second, the names "Chronicles" and "Chronicler's History" imply that the book was written as or purports to be an official record in the nature of annals or the like. As we will see, this impression does not accurately represent the original genre of the work. Third, the name "Chronicler's History" implies that the books of Chronicles and Ezra-Nehemiah are a unit. Again, as we will see below, while these books may be unified at some level, their relationship is much more complicated than is conveyed by this designation.

As suggested by the nomenclature "Chronicler's History," the books of 1-2 Chronicles and Ezra-Nehemiah have long been viewed as being, in some sense, a single work. As with 1-2 Samuel and 1-2 Kings, 1-2 Chronicles is actually a single book — a single book in two volumes, if you will. Ezra and Nehemiah, as we will see, are probably not two separate books but a single work, as indicated by their designation as Ezra-Nehemiah. In addition, Chronicles and Ezra-Nehemiah are clearly linked by the Cyrus edict, which occurs at the end of the former (2 Chr 36:22-23) and the beginning of the latter (Ezra 1:1-4).

The Babylonian Talmud (*Baba Batra* 15a) records the traditional view that Chronicles and Ezra-Nehemiah were written by Ezra. However, in 1832, a scholar named Leopold Zunz reversed the tradition by ascribing Ezra-Nehemiah to the anonymous author of Chronicles and designating the two works together as the "Chronicler's History."[10] Zunz's theory became established in biblical scholarship as the accepted view until the late 1960s and 1970s — roughly the same time that Cross and Smend were publishing their revisions of Noth's DtrH hypothesis. The two scholars whose contributions, in both cases resulting from their doctoral dissertations, brought an end to the consensus surrounding Zunz's theory of common authorship were Sara Japhet and Hugh Williamson.[11]

The case for authorial unity was based on four considerations: (1) the repetition of the Cyrus edict, mentioned earlier; (2) the Apocryphal or Deuterocanonical book of 1 Esdras, which incorporates 2 Chronicles 35–36 and Ezra 1–10 + Nehemiah 8 into a single work; (3) similarities between Chronicles and Ezra-Nehemiah in language and style; and (4) a common theological and ideological outlook between the two books. Japhet and Williamson called into question the last two items. Japhet argued that differences in spelling, vocabulary, and style precluded common authorship and suggested that Chronicles was written later than Ezra-Nehemiah. Williamson focused on the "all Israel" motif in Chronicles, contending that its interest in including the northern tribes among the chosen people of Israel

---

10. Leopold Zunz, *Die gottesdienstlichen Vorträge der Juden* (Berlin: Asher, 1832).

11. Sara Japhet, "The Supposed Common Authorship of Chronicles and Ezra-Nehemiah Investigated Anew," *VT* 18 (1968) 330-71; H. G. M. Williamson, *Israel in the Books of Chronicles* (Cambridge: Cambridge University Press, 1977).

contrasted with the narrowness of Ezra-Nehemiah, which regarded true Israel as exclusively the returnees of the tribes of Judah and Benjamin.

In the decades since the initial salvos of Japhet and Williamson there has been a great deal of scholarly discussion on the question of the authorship of Chronicles-Ezra-Nehemiah. An accurate synthesis of this discussion would have to conclude that, while the final result is inconclusive, the scales are presently tipped in favor of the position that Chronicles and Ezra-Nehemiah were originally separate works by different authors. Following is an attempt to synthesize the discussion on each of the four considerations mentioned above.

(1) The repetition of the Cyrus edict could just as easily be a secondary addition in one or both of the books by an editor who sought to link them editorially as it could the work of a single author.

(2) Scholars debate the nature of 1 Esdras. Is it a fragment of an older, longer work that included both Chronicles and Ezra-Nehemiah in their earlier form as a single book? Or is it a later, independent composition that borrowed materials from Chronicles and Ezra-Nehemiah and revised them for its own purposes? While 1 Esdras appears, on first glance, both to begin and end in the middle of sentences, some recent analysis has contended that both its beginning and its ending are deliberate and not the result of fragmentation. Moreover, several reexaminations of the book in recent years have concluded that it is a composition in its own right, built around the tale of the three youths in 3:1–5:6, and neither the fragment of a longer work nor a simple compilation of materials from Chronicles-Ezra-Nehemiah, though it certainly borrows from these books.[12]

(3) Japhet's results have also not gone uncontested. Some scholars have claimed that the results change when certain presumed source materials are excluded from consideration. Others admit that Japhet showed that linguistic analysis did not demonstrate common authorship. But they add that, at the same time, Japhet did not prove separate authorship on linguistic grounds either. Finally, some scholars have sought to strengthen Japhet's case by considering evidence from compositional techniques and narrative structure, which they find to vary significantly from Chronicles to Ezra-Nehemiah.

12. See Steven L. McKenzie, "The Chronicler as Redactor," in *The Chronicler as Author: Studies in Text and Texture,* ed. M. Patrick Graham and McKenzie, 70-90, esp. 71-78. JSOTSup 263 (Sheffield: Sheffield Academic, 1999).

(4) The recognition of differences in ideology has broadened since Williamson's pioneering work. Scholars have pointed to a number of other themes in Chronicles that are represented differently or not at all in Ezra-Nehemiah. These include the Davidic covenant, the doctrine of immediate punishment for sin or reward for righteousness, marriage to foreigners, the role of prophets, and the exodus.

Thus, while none of these matters is entirely conclusive, the latter three, and particularly the differences in theology and ideology, have led many, if not most, scholars these days to believe that the two books were written by different authors.

Some scholars have offered compromise positions to explain both the similarities and the differences, proposing for instance that Chronicles and Ezra-Nehemiah were written by the same author but as separate books at different times. Cross posited a complex redactional theory, comparable to his proposal for the DtrH, whereby Chronicles-Ezra-Nehemiah developed in stages through the accretion of blocks of material. His theory depends on the assumption that 1 Esdras is a fragment of an older, more extensive work. It has not had the same impact on scholarship as his theory regarding the DtrH. Nevertheless, some kind of editorial link between Chronicles and Ezra-Nehemiah remains a distinct possibility, not only because of the repetition of the Cyrus edict but also because the first three chapters of Ezra evince the strongest similarity to and continuity with Chronicles. Still, scholars have yet to determine the precise nature of the link between the two books.

The distinct authorship of Chronicles and Ezra-Nehemiah may also be indicated by their respective places in the canon. As indicated in the previous chapter, both books are among the Writings, the last and generally latest section of the Hebrew Bible. In fact, while Chronicles' place in the canon was not rigidly fixed — some medieval Bibles placing it first among the Writings or ahead of Ezra-Nehemiah — it is usually the very last book. Certainly that is the case with modern printed editions of the Hebrew Bible. Its ending, encouraging the journeying to Jerusalem to rebuild the temple (2 Chr 36:23), seems an appropriate conclusion to Hebrew Scripture (contrast the ending of the Christian Old Testament, following the LXX, in Mal 4:5-6, which looks forward to the coming of "Elijah" as the Messiah's precursor). Chronicles' place at or near the end of the canon is suggested, incidentally, by Jesus' reference to Zechariah (Matt 23:35; Luke 11:50-51; cf. 2 Chr 24:20-22) as the last of the Hebrew Bible martyrs. This means that Ezra-Nehemiah usually precedes Chronicles, suggesting that it has not traditionally been understood as the latter's sequel.

In view of the likelihood that Chronicles and Ezra-Nehemiah are separate works, certain introductory matters are best treated in detail separately but can be sketched generally here in deference to the grouping of these works as the Chronicler's History and in parallel with our treatment of the DtrH. For instance, the date that one assigns to the Chronicler's History depends on which view of authorship one adopts. If one assumes common authorship in their present form, then both books must be placed after the missions of Ezra and Nehemiah, 444 B.C.E. if Ezra preceded Nehemiah and 398 according to the late date for Ezra. If they are separate works or are viewed as having developed in redactional stages, then Chronicles may be dated earlier. The earliest possible date for Chronicles is 539, based on its reference to Persia and the Cyrus edict (2 Chr 36:20, 22-23), assuming it is not a later addition. However, much later dates are probable, and both Chronicles and Ezra-Nehemiah are usually dated to the fourth century, with Ezra-Nehemiah likely having been written first.

As concerns the genre and purpose of these two affiliated works, Ezra-Nehemiah seems fairly easy to characterize, Chronicles much less so. Ezra-Nehemiah recounts the missions of its two namesakes to Jerusalem. It is, in that sense, history writing. But there is also a theological purpose behind its recounting of the past. That is, it does not simply tell history for history's sake. Rather, the work has a very positive purpose in that it shows that Yahweh has not abandoned his people, despite their past sinfulness and the disaster of the exile. It seeks to demonstrate the renewal and continuity of certain of Israel's traditions, above all the temple and the holy city of Jerusalem, with the past. At the same time, it seeks to point the way forward through the process of self-definition and determination to guard against the kind of misbehavior that led to the exile in the first place. Thus, the book's emphasis on separating the returnees as "true Israel" apart from the corrupt "people of the land," even to the point of mandating divorces, seeks to maintain the ethnic identity and religious purity of Yahweh's chosen people.

Like the DtrH and Ezra-Nehemiah, Chronicles is a written narrative of Israel's national past and thus fits the general contours of the definition of history writing adopted in the previous chapter. Also, like the DtrH and Ezra-Nehemiah, Chronicles does not recount history for history's sake; its interests are predominately theological. But Chronicles is in many ways a unique work with a number of distinctive features. For one thing, Chronicles begins with the longest genealogy on record for Israel (1 Chronicles 1–9). Then, its narrative account of history is borrowed primarily from other biblical writings, which have been at different times quoted, adapted, abbreviated, or supplemented for didactic purposes. The past, or at least part of it, is idealized and presented as paradigmatic. For these reasons, Chronicles has been referred to variously as midrash, exegesis, homily, and propaganda, none of which fully captures all of the work's dimensions. In terms of genre, it is best characterized, at least provisionally as a working definition, as history writing (or perhaps rewriting). But its purpose seems to be especially that of providing theological instruction or furnishing a model for the future drawn from a particular vision of the past.

The studies of Japhet and Williamson mentioned above not only reopened the question of the authorship of Chronicles-Ezra-Nehemiah, but also ushered in a new era of interest in and appreciation for this literature. Prior to their studies, Chronicles-Ezra-Nehemiah were largely ignored by scholars, discounted not only for their historical value but also for their literary worth and theological sophistication. This tendency has been reversed in recent decades. In the more detailed chapters on Chronicles and Ezra-Nehemiah we will see how and why in-depth study of these books has intrigued and excited recent generations of biblical scholars.

3

Methods and Approaches to the Historical Books

On first glance, reading and understanding the Historical Books would seem to be a relatively straightforward enterprise. They are typically and traditionally read as a record of Israel's past. As indicated in the previous chapters, however, such a straightforward reading is complicated by questions of genre brought on by evidence that the contents of these books are not entirely historical. The previous two chapters also described various efforts to understand the authorship and development of the Historical Books and their relationship to each other and to surrounding literature in the Bible. Such efforts reflect both the complex nature of the Historical Books and the variety of methods and approaches that have been developed to try to interpret them.

As noted in Chapter Two above, biblical scholarship as an academic discipline is a product of the Enlightenment, though its roots are far older. It is important to emphasize that biblical scholarship did not begin outside of faith communities but within them. That is, those who first pointed out historical and literary problems within the Bible, particularly the Historical Books, were not nonreligious individuals searching for discrepancies but clergy and persons of faith who noticed such matters precisely because they were reading the Bible very carefully.

Biblical scholarship has continued to be, in essence, the art of reading the Bible carefully or closely. In the course of its development as a discipline, it has fostered a number of methods or approaches to the Bible that read carefully with certain, specific issues or topics in mind. These are typically referred to as "criticisms" or "critical methods or approaches," the word "critical/criticism" being used in the sense not of finding fault but of careful analysis. This book will employ a variety of approaches or methods depending on the book or passage under consideration, since some methods are more suited for analyzing certain passages or kinds of literature than others. The remainder of this chapter will survey the critical methods to be used in our analyses of the Historical Books. This does not represent a list or discussion of all the methods available to scholars, but only those deemed to be most useful and of greatest interest to readers of this volume.[1] I will use the famous story of David and Goliath in 1 Samuel 17 for purposes of illustration of how these different methods work to aid our understanding of the Historical Books.

Diachronic Methods

Academic methods of Bible study are of two basic kinds: diachronic and synchronic. Diachronic methods are also referred to as historical-critical and synchronic as literary-critical. As the names imply, diachronic methods are concerned with the relationship of the biblical materials to history. They also attempt to trace the development of the biblical literature through time. Synchronic methods, by contrast, concentrate on the literature as such — the artistry and interrelationships within the biblical text as we have it, regardless of how it came to be.

Textual Criticism[2]

Textual criticism helps to illustrate the difference between diachronic and synchronic approaches. Since its goal is to establish the text to be analyzed,

1. For a broad introduction to the varieties of methods of critical study of the Bible, see Steven L. McKenzie and Stephen R. Haynes, eds., *To Each Its Own Meaning: An Introduction to Biblical Criticisms and Their Application*, 2nd ed. (Louisville: Westminster John Knox, 1999).

2. There has been a great deal written about textual criticism in recent decades. However, two still eminently useful introductions to the topic are Ralph W. Klein, *Textual Criticism of the Old Testament: The Septuagint after Qumran*. GBS (Philadelphia: Fortress, 1974); and P. Kyle McCarter, *Textual Criticism: Recovering the Text of the Hebrew Bible*. GBS (Philadelphia: Fortress, 1986).

it might be considered a preliminary step to both diachronic and synchronic work. But the text that it seeks to establish is the original one penned by the author before it became altered or "corrupted" through transmission by scribes copying and recopying it. That is obviously a diachronic enterprise. Synchronic methods tend to be interested not in the text as the author(s) produced it but in the text as it is encountered by readers, however it may have evolved. Practically, therefore, synchronic critics rarely engage in textual criticism.

Textual criticism is also sometimes called "lower criticism," dealing with the text's transmission, in distinction to the other "higher critical" methods, which we will discuss momentarily, that concern the text's composition. However, this distinction is artificial; composition and transmission were not always distinct activities, as the example of 1 Samuel 17 will show.

The need for textual criticism is occasioned by the fact that we do not possess the original version (the "autograph") of any of the books of the Bible. What we have instead are manuscripts that are the product of generations of transmission of the biblical books through copying and recopying by scribes. Although highly trained, these scribes worked without the benefit of such modern aids as eyeglasses and electric lights. Unintentional errors were inevitable. Variant readings multiplied over the centuries, producing a diverse set of texts and text types for some books of the Bible. This diversity was quelled in the late first or early second century C.E. by the establishment of a kind of "official" or received text *(textus receptus)* for each biblical book. It was this text that was then preserved and edited — in the sense of fixing spellings, adding aids for the reader, and the like — by families of Jewish scribes in the first millennium C.E. and that now serves as the basis for printed editions of the Hebrew Bible. This received text is known as the Masoretic Text (MT), from the Hebrew word *masorah,* meaning "tradition." However, the former diversity of the text has been made clear by the discovery of the Dead Sea Scrolls, which have, in turn, affirmed the value of the Septuagint (the Greek translation of the Old Testament, abbreviated LXX) as a textual witness.

To explain this complicated situation in other terms, printed editions of the Hebrew Bible today are typically based on one of two codices named after the cities in which they were found. (A codex is an early form of book, usually with pages of parchment instead of paper.) The Aleppo Codex dates from about 900 C.E. and the Leningrad Codex around 1000 C.E. The book of 1 Samuel as part of the Deuteronomistic History was probably written around 560 B.C.E., as we saw in Chapter Two above. Thus, our fullest manuscripts for 1 Samuel — and this is representative of the situation for all the books of the Hebrew Bible — are some fifteen hundred years later than the composition of the books themselves!

This lengthy gap in time highlights the enormous importance of the Dead Sea Scrolls for textual criticism of the Hebrew Bible. Copied in the period between ca. 250 B.C.E. and 68 C.E., they are roughly one thousand years earlier than the best Hebrew manuscripts known before their discovery. First discovered in 1946-47, the Dead Sea Scrolls have revolutionized our understanding of the text of the Hebrew Bible. They attest the variety of Hebrew texts in existence at the turn of the eras that had arisen through the copying and recopying of the biblical books since those books were composed. They also showed that the LXX, which was translated in the third century B.C.E., can be a valuable witness to the Hebrew text it renders into Greek. In the case of 1-2 Samuel, for instance, the LXX translation is very literal, making it relatively easy to reconstruct a Hebrew forebear. Remarkably, the Dead Sea Scrolls fragments of Samuel proved to be closer to the Hebrew text behind the LXX than to the MT, which had served as the basis for the Hebrew Bible for so long.

The Dead Sea Scrolls material varies from book to book. Likewise, the value of the LXX is not the same for all of the biblical books. This makes textual criticism a complicated endeavor. Still, textual criticism should not be ignored (though it often is). The text and how it reads is, after all, fundamental for consideration of any other aspect of biblical literature — what it means, how it developed, its aesthetic value, etc. In a volume like the present one it will be impossible to conduct a thorough text-critical analysis of each of the Historical Books. However, there are places where textual criticism plays a particularly significant role, and we will concentrate on these. One such place is the story of David and Goliath in 1 Samuel 17.

In 1 Samuel 17, and carrying over into ch. 18, the LXX is significantly shorter than the MT, lacking vv. 12-31, 50, 55-58 and 18:1-5. That these verses are secondary is indicated by two considerations. First, the shorter LXX version presents a consistent story in its own right. Second, additional verses cause inconsistencies and contradictions in the present Hebrew narrative. For instance, as that narrative now has it, David actually kills Goliath twice! In v. 50, he kills him with a sling stone; then, in v. 51, he kills him again by beheading. The secondary nature of 18:1-5 is particularly obvious.

The next verse (18:6, "As they were coming home, when David returned from killing the Philistine . . .") is clearly the immediate continuation of the story in ch. 17 and does not allow for the passage of time required for David's military successes described in 18:5. In short, the LXX is a better version of this story and shows that the received Hebrew text has been expanded by one or more other versions of the tale.

There are also other, more detailed instances in this story where textual criticism can help to shape understanding. In 17:4, Goliath is famously described as being six cubits and a span — something like nine and one-half feet — in height. The LXX reads *four* cubits and a span, or about six and one-half feet. The larger number is suspicious because of the tendency in a legendary story like this one to expand such details. In addition, the number "six" occurs below in the description of Goliath's spear (v. 7) and might have furnished the source for the mistaken replacement of the original "four" through the unconscious eye skip of a scribe.

Literary (Source) Criticism

This method was formerly known as literary criticism. But since that name is also used for synchronic, literary-critical methods, the term "source criticism" avoids ambiguity. Source criticism grew out of observations by careful readers of phenomena in the Pentateuch, especially Genesis, indicating the presence of material by more than one author. Basically, a reader exercising source criticism looks for four kinds of phenomena: (1) tensions, inconsistencies, or contradictions within a text or between texts; (2) repetitions or duplications that are not part of an author's style or integral to the narrative; (3) changes in vocabulary, writing style, and outlook; (4) interruptions and breaks in a text's continuity. Source criticism assumes that such phenomena are best accounted for by postulating originally different writers or documents. A more specific kind of source criticism that is especially relevant for the Historical Books focuses on the process by which a text or book is formed out of constituent sources — e.g., an author using sources or an editor combining them. This approach is known as "redaction criticism."

Applying source critical criteria to 1 Samuel 17, we can find instances of each of the phenomena listed above. First, there are tensions or inconsistencies within the narrative. We have already noticed one of the most glaring of these involving whether David killed Goliath with the sling or a sword (vv. 50-51). Another such problem arises with Saul's question at the end of the story, "Whose son are you?" (v. 58). This is an idiom for "Who are you?" indicating that Saul does not know David or anything about him. Yet 16:14-23, which portions of ch. 17 presume, makes clear that Saul knows both David, with whom he has a close relationship, and David's father, from whom he requested David as his armor-bearer (16:21-22).

The twofold slaying of Goliath might also be considered a repetition. There are additional repetitions. For instance, Goliath is introduced twice (17:4 and 23), the only two times, in fact, that he is called by name in the story. David is also introduced in v. 12 as though it were his first appearance, despite the reader's familiarity with him from ch. 16.

The changes in writing style and outlook are more subtle. The best example is probably the depiction of David. While David is referred to as a youth throughout the story, parts of ch. 17 (especially vv. 12-31) cast him as younger and more inexperienced than the rest of the chapter. Thus, while 17:1-11, 32-49 depict him, in line with the end of ch. 16, as being Saul's full-time armor-bearer, in vv. 12-31 he is still a shepherd who serves as a messenger boy going back and forth between his father and his brothers in the army (vv. 15, 20). In addition, Goliath's defiance is constant and ongoing over a forty-day period (v. 16) rather than a onetime challenge (v. 10).

Finally, we have already noticed 18:1-5 as the best example of an interruption in the narrative. These verses break the continuity between the story of David and Goliath and the events immediately following (18:6-9) by reporting on David's relationship with Jonathan and his protracted military success.

These observations show, as mentioned earlier, that the separation between lower (textual) and higher criticism can be artificial. Composition and transmission were not always distinct activities. The text of the Hebrew Bible was sometimes composed during the process of transmission, as in 1 Samuel 17. Here, source-critical conclusions are supported by text-critical ones, indicating that the MT is composite, and a significant portion of the present account (17:12-31, 50, 55-58 and 18:1-5) was added secondarily to an older version of the story preserved in the LXX.

In addition to indicating tensions within the narrative of 1 Samuel 17, source-critical observations also point to inconsistencies between this story and the materials that presently surround it. For example, whatever age David is supposed to be in ch. 17, he is obviously young and has no experience as a warrior. Yet he is described in 16:18 as a "man of war." Then, at the end of the story, David is said to have taken Goliath's head to Jerusalem and kept his armor in his tent (17:54). The reference to his tent, incidentally, is another tension within the chapter, since according to v. 15, David did not stay with the army but shuttled back and forth between his father and his brothers. Beyond that, though, the reference to Jerusalem here appears anachronistic, since the larger narrative assumes that the city remained in Jebusite hands and was not conquered by David until after his anointing as king over Israel (2 Sam 5:6-10). The mention of Goliath's armor being in David's tent also seems to be in tension with a later story that locates the Philistine's sword with the priests who guard the ark (1 Sam 21:8-9). These inconsistencies may suggest that the story of David and Goliath was once an independent tale, separate and distinct from the larger narrative about David.

Form Criticism

Form criticism studies the Bible by concentrating on its literary types or genres. The assumption behind this method is that discerning a text's type or genre is crucial to understanding its purpose and meaning. Thus, it makes a great difference whether a person approaches a particular book or film as history as opposed to, say, science fiction.

Unfortunately, there are no firm rules for determining genre, as it is a cultural phenomenon. Types of literature vary from culture to culture, and people within a given culture learn how to distinguish its different genres in much the same way as they "absorb" a language simply by growing up in that culture. Still, as with languages, there are rules or guidelines signaling different genres. Some of these involve physical form. In our culture, letters, newspaper articles, and research papers come in different forms that are easily distinguishable. In antiquity, there were also physical differences between documents like letters and royal decrees. Such physical differences have disappeared, however, in the Bible's collection of works, and the differences between genres must now be discerned by internal clues. The documents that have been preserved from the ancient world help us to know what those internal clues are. Often, they come at the beginning or ending of a document, just as "Dateline, New York" opens a news report and

INTRODUCTION TO THE HISTORICAL BOOKS

"They lived happily ever after" concludes a fairy tale. Creative authors may combine or mix genres, playing with their audience's expectations, in order to get a point across, as was discussed in Chapter One of this book.

Form criticism basically consists of four related concerns or steps. The first is the discernment of a text's structure, particularly where it begins and where it ends, but also the way in which its constituent elements are distinguished and arranged. Form criticism may be applied to a single passage, an entire book, or even a larger, extended work. The discussions of the Historical Books and of the Deuteronomistic History and Chronicler's History in the previous two chapters reflected form-critical analysis. In the case of 1 Samuel 17, a new episode obviously begins in v. 1 with the notice of the Philistines gathering for battle. The introduction of David in v. 12 indicates the beginning of a separate narrative. The reference to the Israelites despoiling the Philistine camp together with the report about what David did with Goliath's head and armor (vv. 53-54) provide an appropriate ending to the story, so that Saul's questioning David about his identity (vv. 55-58) appears extraneous.

As for the chapter's internal structure and content, the reader is led to expect David's response immediately following the Philistine's challenge and the report that Saul and all Israel were afraid (17:10-11), so that the reintroduction of David and description of his interaction with Eliab (vv. 12-31) again seems extraneous. Saul's wish for David's success (v. 37) seems a fitting conclusion to their interview before David goes into action. This might suggest that the episode about Saul trying his armor on David (vv. 38-40) is additional to the bare story and designed to add some element to the point of the story. David's exchange with Goliath (vv. 43-47) might be a typical feature of battle reports, as there are other examples of "trash talking" for purposes of "psyching out" an opponent in an imminent military engagement (cf. 2 Kings 18). The length and content of David's speech, however, suggests that the author is making a theological statement. The remaining ingredients in the narrative are all expected — i.e., reports of David's victory, pursuit by the Israelites, and plundering of the Philistines. The only unusual feature, as we have seen, is the double account of Goliath's death (vv. 50-51).

The second step in a form-critical investigation is determining a text's genre. Since there is no official catalogue of ancient genres, this is best done by a process of intuition and elimination. The DtrH is probably best characterized as history writing, as we have seen, but its constituent parts are of many different genres. I have referred to 1 Samuel 17 as story and as legend. The latter is probably the best descriptor of its genre, if it is defined as a story focused on a personality of special religious or political significance that had its origin in oral tradition and grew and developed over time. It is worth noting in this regard that there is nothing physically impossible about what David does in this story — no direct intervention of God or explicitly miraculous element. The focus is on David's personal qualities, his extraordinary faith and trust in God. It is clear, moreover, from the fact that the Hebrew version of the story is conflated that it developed over time, with David growing younger and less inexperienced with warfare.

Third, hand-in-hand with the definition of genre is the determination of the life setting out of which a text arose and in which it was used. This consideration is more important for certain texts and genres than for others. Some psalms, for instance, may have had a setting in liturgical worship. Laments may have arisen from funerals. There is a great deal more uncertainty about a text like 1 Samuel 17, and we can only hazard a guess. The legendary nature of the story suggests that it likely served to praise and promote David as a national and military hero. The quintessential victory of the underdog may have resonated strongly with Israel as a small country caught between the great imperial powers of its day — Egypt, Assyria, Babylonia, Persia. As such, the story may well have been popular as entertainment. The story may even have been used in educational or religious settings to reinforce the values of belief in and reliance on divine protection and courage stemming from belief and faith.

The final step in form criticism is trying to discern the purpose of a text or, in other words, the author's intent behind writing it. This is again something that must be inferred or deduced most of the time. Comparison with other texts of the same genre can be especially helpful. The story in 1 Samuel 17 seems intended to present David as an ideal young man, a model of faith and courage. As such, its purpose is almost certainly didactic, at least in part. In its present setting especially, the story illustrates David's character in preparation for the following narratives about him and his leadership. It may be fair to say that this is the kind of heroic legend that idealizes David as Israel's greatest king and the embodiment of its national spirit in much the same way as stories about Washington or Lincoln do vis-à-vis the United States and Americans.

A branch of form criticism that is especially important for the Historical Books is known as "tradition history" or "tradition-historical criticism." As its name implies, tradition history seeks to trace the history of a tradition from its origin to its current presentation in the Bible. It may be thought of not as a separate method alongside textual, source, form, and other criticisms, but as an approach that attempts to synthesize the results of all of these methods into a full picture of a tradition's development and use. Tradition history may focus on a single text or story, attempting to trace its history from its earliest inception to its present written state in the Hebrew Bible. Or it may study how a tradition is used in different ways by several biblical texts and try to trace a development in the relationship of those texts.

A consideration of the David and Goliath tradition would probably have to begin with the question of whether and to what extent the story is based on history, particularly in view of 2 Sam 21:19, which credits someone else with killing Goliath. It might try to show, among other things, how this popular tale grew over time, both orally and in writing, how different versions of it developed, how the author of 1 Samuel 17 adapted it to fit the larger David story, and how in the transmission of the text elements from another version of the story crept in. A broader tradition history would step outside of 1 Samuel 17 and discuss the allusions to the David and Goliath tradition in other texts, both in Samuel (1 Sam 21:9; 22:10; perhaps 25:29) and in other biblical books (1 Chr 20:5) including Psalm 151 contained in the LXX.

Historical Reconstruction

The methods just surveyed all stand, to a lesser or greater extent, in the service of what is the ultimate goal of historical criticism — determining the extent to which the biblical materials reflect or convey actual history. Naturally, this is an especially important matter in the Historical Books. In addition to these analytical methods, the biblical historian has other tools at her or his disposal. Two of the most important of these are texts from other, especially ancient Near Eastern, sources, and archaeology. Both are seldom unambiguous. That is, they require as much interpretation as the Bible. Archaeology, in particular, has changed a great deal in recent decades. No longer is it a treasure expedition *a la* Indiana Jones. Big ticket discoveries are rare. The focus of newer archaeology is on the daily existence of common folk rather than single events and major figures, such as kings. It is interested in long-range environmental and economic changes and their impact on entire cultures and societies. Archaeology today is especially influenced by anthropology, which studies different societies and cultures looking for patterns in how human organizations arise and develop. This approach is especially relevant for the Historical Books, which relate such developments as the transition of Israel to nationhood under the institution of monarchy.

When it comes to specific events in the Bible, rarely is it possible to demonstrate that they happened as described. That is certainly so for the story of David and Goliath. The very existence of David as a historical person has been intensely debated among scholars. A recently-discovered inscription containing the first attestation of his name outside of the Bible seems to have convinced most scholars that he did exist. Even so, the name occurs in the expression "house of David," referring to the kingdom of Judah or its ruling house, and tells nothing of David's life or person. Similarly, an inscription containing a name similar to Goliath shows only that such names, already known from Greek sources, were in use among the Philistines in the tenth-ninth century. Goliath's armor as described in 1 Sam 17:5-7 appears to be a compilation of different arms from different cultures and different periods. Rather than having any historical value, it serves the literary function of showing that David's Philistine opponent was "armed to the teeth." The sling is well attested as a serious military weapon throughout ancient Near Eastern history. Its use to strike effectively from long range is a realistic element in the story. In short, the story of David's victory with a sling over a larger and better armed opponent is plausible. But there are reasons to believe that, if it did happen, it did not take place exactly as described in 1 Samuel 17, as indicated by the internal source, form, and tradition-historical issues treated above, including the attribution of the victory to someone other than David in 2 Sam 21:19.

Synchronic Methods

If diachronic methods explore the vertical depth of the text as it developed over time, synchronic methods explore the horizontal richness that it presents to readers. Put another way, diachronic methods concentrate on the side of text production — the interaction of authors, editors, and tradents with the text. Synchronic methods, by contrast, focus on the other side of the communication equation — the interaction of readers with the text.

Canonical Criticism

In addition to being, in some sense, history and literature, the Bible is also Scripture. This acknowledgement is fundamental for canonical criticism. With a text's final form as its starting point, this method seeks to understand how that text relates to the larger body of Scripture — Jewish or Christian — of which it is a part. Canonical criticism studies the ways in which biblical texts were authoritative for faith communities, how they helped to shape those communities and were in turn invested by them with new meaning. Canonical criticism shares interests with several other approaches to the Bible. Its concern with how canonical texts were used by faith communities is reminiscent of tradition history. Its interest in how texts within the Bible relate to one another overlaps with an approach referred to as "intertextuality," the main difference being that canonical criticism is focused more on the canon as an entity.

As one of the introductory texts to the David story, 1 Samuel 17 helps to influence the way that the narrative about David is read. First and foremost, it shows his trust in Yahweh in times of challenge and crisis — a trait he will continue to demonstrate throughout Samuel. The story displays his courage and military expertise and his willingness to "go to bat" on behalf of his people and against their enemies who defy their God. As such, this tale presents David as a model of leadership, a role he continues to hold for the rest of the account of the histories of Israel and Judah in 1-2 Kings. David's piety and faith as exemplified in our chapter are crucial ingredients of his model leadership and contribute to the image of David beyond the DtrH in works like Chronicles and Psalms. Beyond that, these traits are essential elements in the expectation of a messiah as the "anointed" heir in the line of David who will save his people from oppression by foreign giants just as David did. In the New Testament and for the Christian community, Jesus is the fulfillment of the messianic hope that is founded in David and is thus given the title "son of David."

A canonical interpretation might take into consideration not only the way in which the story of David and Goliath contributed to the David figure in the Hebrew Bible and New Testament as a whole but also how that figure influences the reading of the story. It is impossible to read the heroic tale without the awareness of what David will become. The qualities of self-assuredness and violence that are the cause of grief in other parts of the story are to be found here in incipient, albeit tempered, form.

Narrative Criticism

In deliberate contrast to diachronic methods, narrative criticism approaches the text as a whole and finds meaning in it through the analysis of such features as plot and structure, characterization, and creative use of language, what some might call the text's rhetoric or aesthetics. Its academic affinities as working paradigms are with the disciplines of English and literary studies rather than history. Modern narrative critics are often subversive or deconstructive, exposing biases and power structures supposedly supported in a text and exploring how a close reading may overturn its surface sense. They can, therefore, have an explicitly and deliberately ideological agenda (e.g., feminist, gay-lesbian, socioeconomic). Typically in narrative analyses, God is treated as a character within the world of the text rather than somehow above or beyond it.

A narratological analysis of the David and Goliath story might locate its meaning in the characterizations of the prime actors, Goliath, David, and Saul. The supposed tensions signaled by diachronic methods might be viewed as the key. The presentation of David in vv. 12-30 contrasts him not only with Goliath but also with Saul. David is "small time," a mere shepherd. His portrayal in this way is likely an allusion to his potential and his future, since kings are often described as shepherds. At this point, though, David is devalued as insignificant not only by his adversary, but also by his family, and Saul. Saul's obtuseness is evident in the comedic scene in vv. 38-39. Having wished David Yahweh's presence and aid (v. 37), he tries to dress David in bulky armor, thereby undermining David's two main weapons of trust in Yahweh and the ability to remain mobile and attack from a distance. Saul and Goliath are exactly alike in their reliance on the external traits of raw strength and weaponry. David rises above them both through his reliance on the inner qualities of courage, ingenuity, and faith.

A more ideological approach might propose an anarchical reading of the story along the following lines. David is demeaned by the power structures within his own society — family and government — as well as external enemies. Friend and foe are identical in this regard. Both Goliath and Saul turn out to be weak and ineffectual because they place their trust in the proliferation of arms. Israel's greatest resources are internal and lie within its citizens. Social and governmental structures perpetuate stereotypes that mask David's valuable talents and inner qualities (16:18). Ironically, this verse describes David as a "man of war," suggesting that he is already being co-opted for participation in the same structures that here bring an end to Goliath and Saul but will eventually cause grief to David himself.

Conclusion

As might be expected, these different methods and approaches sometimes produce different results. Two points are worth recognizing here. First, all methods are merely means to the end, that end being the understanding of the biblical material. Second, it may well be the case that, at least sometimes, there is no single "right" understanding of a biblical book or passage. This is not to challenge the notion of the Bible's truth or authority. But the idea that the Bible can be understood in different ways or has different meanings to different people or even to the same person at different times is certainly not a new one. The reward of these approaches to the Bible is that they guide readers and help them to examine the biblical text carefully. That is the primary goal of this book. Hence, in the discussion of the Historical Books in the following chapters, I will make use of different methods at different times and synthesize the conclusions of scholars using different approaches. However, since this book is not a primer in the use of different methods, I do not always specify the particular method used to reach a given conclusion, but leave that to the discernment of the reader.

4

Joshua

The book of Joshua has been aptly called a "canonical hinge."[1] It comes immediately after the Pentateuch (Genesis–Deuteronomy) and is at the head of the Former Prophets. It relates the acquisition and apportionment of the land of Canaan, which is the fulfillment of the promise to the patriarchs and the objective of the people who experienced the exodus from Egypt and the wilderness wanderings. That same land is also the setting of the story of the nation of Israel narrated in the rest of the Former Prophets. Joshua, the main hero of the book, is the successor of Moses and the forerunner of the judges and kings who subsequently lead Israel.

Content and Structure

Perusal of Joshua reveals that the book has two main halves: the conquest of the land in chs. 1–12 and the division of it among the tribes in chs. 13–24. Closer examination indicates subdivisions within these halves. The first five chapters focus on Israel's preparations for conquest, while chs. 6–12 recount the conquest itself. Then, chs. 13–21 detail the boundaries of the tribal divisions, while chs. 22–24 provide a kind of epilogue to the book, with ch. 22 relating an anecdote about misunderstanding between the tribes on either side of the Jordan and chs. 23–24 giving two speeches by

---

1. L. Daniel Hawk, "Joshua, Book of," *DOTHB*, 563.

Joshua. The latter three chapters, especially the speeches, convey warnings about the future and the necessity for continued obedience. The book, therefore, can be outlined broadly as follows:

Joshua 1–12: Conquest of Canaan
        1–5: Prologue: preparations for conquest
        6–12: Conquering the land

Joshua 13–24: Division of Canaan
        13–21: Dividing the land among the tribes
        22–24: Epilogue: the need for continuing obedience

Within this broad outline, there are signs of further deliberate structuring. Thus, the commission of Joshua at the beginning of the book (1:1–9) is matched by the notice of his death near the end (24:29-31). The list of kings defeated by the Israelites on both sides of the Jordan in ch. 12 provides a kind of summary of the conquest in the first half of the book. The notices about Joshua's advanced age (13:1; 23:1) bracket the account of the division of the land. The allotment to the "other tribes" (apart from the "main" tribes of Judah, Ephraim, and western Manasseh) is framed by an introduction and conclusion (18:1; 19:51). The latter verse does double duty as a frame also for the whole section of allotment of the land west of the Jordan (14:1-5; 19:51). This material boasts a further inner frame in the form of special allotments to the two faithful spies, Caleb (14:6-15) and Joshua (19:49-50).

Coordinating with the literary structure of the book is an arrangement according to geographical location. The conquest focuses first on the central part of Canaan with the fall of Jericho and Ai (chs. 6–8) and the ruse of the Gibeonites (ch. 9). The focus then turns south (ch. 10) and then north (ch. 11), culminating in the destruction of Hazor. Similarly, the second half of the book describes the division of the land east of the Jordan among the two and one-half tribes of Reuben, Gad, and half-Manasseh (ch. 13). It then moves to the west with the inheritance of Judah (chs. 14–15) and the "Joseph" tribes of Ephraim and the other half of Manasseh (chs. 16–17). The allotments to the rest of the tribes come next (chs. 18–19), followed by the listing of the cities of refuge (ch. 20) and the cities designated for the Levites throughout the territories of the other tribes (ch. 21).

A detailed outline of Joshua, then, looks like this:

Joshua

Conquest of Canaan: Joshua 1–12

Prologue: Preparations for conquest (Josh 1–5)

1   Commissions
   1:1–9   Commissioning of Joshua
   1:10-11   Joshua orders the people to prepare to cross the Jordan
   1:12-18   Transjordan tribes to help conquer the territory west of the Jordan

2   Rahab and the spies

3–4   Crossing the Jordan

5   Ritual preparations
   5:1-9   General circumcision
   5:10-12   Keeping Passover
   5:13-15   The commander of Yahweh's army appears to Joshua

Conquering the land (Josh 6–12)

6   Conquest of Jericho

7   Achan's sin

8   Conquest of Ai
   8:1-29   Fall of Ai
   8:30-35   Covenant renewal at Shechem

9   Gibeonites' ruse

10   Defeat of coalition of southern kings and conquest of southern cities

11   Conquest of the north
   11:1-15   Defeat of northern kings
   11:16-23   Summaries: Joshua took the whole land

12   List of defeated kings
   12:1-6   Kings east of the Jordan
   12:7-24   Kings west of the Jordan

Division of Canaan: Joshua 13–24

Dividing the land among the tribes (Josh 13–21)

13:1-7   Prelude: The land that remains to be conquered
13:8-33   Allotment to the transjordanian tribes

41

Composition and Growth

The authorship of this book is traditionally ascribed to Joshua himself. However, scholars almost universally discount this ascription, and for good reason. Careful reading reveals plenty of evidence of literary unevenness suggesting that the book had a long and complicated compositional history. Some of the more obvious examples of literary unevenness are hinted at in the outline. Some passages state or at least imply that Israel conquered the entire land and had rest from warfare (10:40-42; 11:16-23; 12:1-24; 21:43-45). These are contradicted by other notices that a significant portion of the land remained to be taken (13:1-7; 15:13-19, 63; 16:10; 17:11-13; 19:47; 23:1-13).

The book also attests several doublets. Joshua seems to give two valedictory addresses (chs. 23; 24). He twice commands the Israelites to choose twelve men, the first time for some unspecified reason (3:12), the second time to carry stones from the midst of the Jordan riverbed (4:3). The stones are deposited both in the campsite (4:8) and in the middle of the Jordan (4:9), and different reasons are given for the stones as memorials (4:6-7, 21-24). The mention of Joshua's age before the allotment lists (13:1) is repeated after them (23:1). There are two references to Caleb receiving Kiriath-arba/Hebron (14:6-15; 15:13-14) and a third indicating that he received the fields and villages around Kiriath-arba/Hebron, but not the city itself, which went to the Levites (21:11-12).

Scholars typically posit different writers and/or different levels of writing in an effort to account for these kinds of literary unevenness. Older scholarship saw in Joshua a continuation of the sources or literary strands identified in the Pentateuch — especially J and P. These scholars spoke and wrote of a *Hexa*teuch rather than a *Penta*teuch, that is, a unit of six scrolls instead of five. This model emphasized the conquest in Joshua as the fulfillment anticipated in and even required by the story in Genesis–Deuteronomy. In very broad terms, the base of the narrative in chs. 2–11 + 24 was assigned to J, the ritual material in chs. 3–6 and the lists in 13–21 to P, and the speeches in chs. 1 and 23 to D editing. The Hexateuch model all but disappeared following the advent of Martin Noth's Deuteronomistic History theory in 1943 (although the idea has experienced a resurgence in recent years). Noth's model emphasized the strong ties between Joshua and Deuteronomy as well as the continuity of Joshua with the subsequent Former Prophets (see Chapter Two above).

Following Noth's basic model, most scholars think of Joshua's development (and that of the other books in the DtrH as well) in three broad stages: pre-Dtr, Dtr, and post-Dtr. The pre-Dtr stage involves the book's original source materials. The book itself names one document, the no-longer-extant Book of Jashar (also cited in 2 Sam 1:18), as the source of the poetic fragment in Josh 10:12-13. Scholars have observed other phenomena that suggest the presence of once independent traditions or documents. Some of the boundary lists in chs. 13–21, for instance, might derive from distinct documents. This could explain why some locations show up in the lists of more than one tribe (e.g., Kiriath-jearim in both Judah [15:60] and

Benjamin [18:28 LXX] and Eshtaol in Judah [15:33] and Dan [19:41]). The tribal lists would then have come from different periods. As for the narratives, most of the traditions in chs. 1–12 are set within the confined territory of Benjamin and the nearby sanctuary of Gilgal. They likely originated in this small, central region, which is portrayed here as representing the whole land of Canaan, at least west of the Jordan. Noth, followed by other scholars, thought that the stories underlying Joshua 2–11 had already been gathered before Dtr into a collection that was preserved and passed on in connection with the cultic activity at Gilgal. The fear and dread of the Canaanite kings before the advancing Israelites is often cited as a major theme of this collection. Even scholars who do not believe that there was such a pre-Dtr collection would agree that Dtr had access to traditions and stories in some form. Most of the etiologies for place names and geographical features likely come from the pre-Dtr level as well.

The Dtr level of Joshua is most evident in a set of speeches in the book that focus on the matter of obedience to the law in Deuteronomy. Joshua's opening speech in 1:1-9 and his farewell address in ch. 23 are widely recognized as Dtr's handiwork, as is the summary in 21:43-45 followed by the speech in 22:1-6. In general, most scholars follow Noth in recognizing Dtr's work in Joshua 1–11 + 23 as material both edited and authored by him, whether he worked with older independent traditions or an already extant collection. As with other books in the DtrH, some scholars believe there was more than one Dtr redactor and explain some of the doublets by appeal to a second level of Dtr working.

Again following Noth, most scholars find ample evidence of post-Dtr additions in the book of Joshua. Above all, the boundary lists in chs. 13–22 and Joshua's second address in ch. 24 are widely considered additions to the Dtr level of the book. This is because Dtr language is largely absent from the boundary lists. The speech in ch. 24 is set in Shechem, which is never mentioned as conquered in chs. 1–11 and lies outside of the central Benjamin-Ephraimite region that is the focus of those chapters. The boundary lists likely were added to the book during the late exilic or Persian period (late sixth or fifth century) and reflect the hope that the people of Israel would repossess its ancestral land. Some scholars have even suggested that the lists are utopian and represent idealized tribal boundaries rather than the actual extent of tribal holdings from any time in the past.

This three-tiered scheme — pre-Dtr, Dtr, and post-Dtr levels — is helpful for gaining some sense of manageability to the very complicated situation behind the development of the book of Joshua. However, scholars are far from agreed when it comes to fitting the specific texts of the book into this scheme. Two examples, one from each half of the book, can illustrate. The first concerns the story of Rahab and the spies in Joshua 2. In its present location, it falls between two references to a three-day period leading up to the crossing of the Jordan (1:11; 3:2). Since the events narrated in ch. 2 take more than three days, that story's disturbance of the chronology indicates that it is an insertion. However, scholars disagree about the developmental stage at which the insertion was made. Some, including Noth, assign the Rahab story to the pre-Dtr level, attributing its insertion to the pre-Dtr collector. Others see the Rahab story as a post-Dtr insertion into Dtr's basic narrative. The matter is complicated by Rahab's speech in 2:9-13. Both positions recognize that the bulk of the speech (vv. 9-11) is patently theological and is part of a "hear and fear" theme running through Joshua 1–11, according to which the kings and people of Canaan are afraid of the Israelites because of what they have heard about Yahweh's deeds on their behalf (5:1; 6:1; 9:1-3; 10:1-2; 11:1-5).[2] Both positions also recognize that these verses contain Dtr elements. Those who hold the view that the story was part of the source collection used by Dtr regard the "hear and fear" motif as a major theme of that collection and the Dtr language as minimal and a later accretion.[3] Those who see the story as a post-Dtr addition argue that the "hear and fear" motif represents a theme of a set of additions to Dtr's account of the conquest in Joshua 1–11 and believe that the Dtr elements in Rahab's speech are imitative of Dtr's language and style.

The second example of complicated development relates to boundary lists in the second half of Joshua. A primary reason that scholars regard these as a later addition is the repeated reference to Joshua's age in 13:1 and 23:1-2. The reference to his old age leads the reader to expect his valedictory speech, which is what takes place in ch. 23. The long account of the division of the land is an unexpected non sequitur following the reference to Joshua's age in 13:1. In other words, the reference to his age in 13:1 leads the reader to expect a speech that does not come until ten chapters later. This is, moreover, a common editorial technique known as "narrative resump-

---

2. The term "hear and fear" and the list here are taken from the notes to Joshua by K. Lawson Younger in the NOAB.

3. Cf. Richard D. Nelson, *Joshua*. OTL (Louisville: Westminster John Knox, 1997) 40-41.

tion," whereby an editor repeats part of the text into which material is inserted immediately before and after the insertion, so that the narrative literally takes up where it left off before the insertion. However, if we assume, with most scholars, that Joshua 13–22 is a post-Dtr insertion, then the passage in 21:43–22:6 presents a problem, because its language and style are widely recognized as Dtr. At the very least, this would mean that the insertion of the boundary lists involved more than a simple narrative resumption. For some scholars, it is an indication that Dtr included the boundary lists in some form or that there was more than one level of Dtr editing.[4]

To conclude this section on composition where we began, scholars are universally agreed that Joshua reflects a complicated history of composition. There is general consensus that its primary connections are with Deuteronomy and the books that follow it in the DtrH. However, it is also undeniable that it shares features with the Pentateuchal books, at least as the fulfillment of their promises of the land of Canaan, if not specifically with the Pentateuchal sources J and P. In recent years, some scholars have attempted to explain this duality of Joshua by postulating the continuation of J and P at a post-Dtr stage, with the boundary divisions in Joshua 13–22 in particular being assigned to P.[5]

Text

NB: Since this section contains some technical terms and abbreviations, it may be useful to the reader to review the section on Textual Criticism in Chapter Three above before proceeding.

The differences between the MT and LXX of Joshua are significant enough that they should be characterized as distinct editions or recensions of the book, especially in certain chapters (Joshua 5; 6; 20; 24). In general, the LXX is shorter and the MT expansionistic, so that the LXX reflects the better text. However, there are cases where the reverse is true, particularly at the end of ch. 24.

The Dead Sea Scrolls include fragments of two manuscripts of the

4. See Adrian H. W. Curtis, *Joshua*. OTG (Sheffield: Sheffield Academic, 1997) 32-35.

5. The presence of J and P in Joshua at a post-Dtr level is a basic contention of John Van Seters, *In Search of History: Historiography in the Ancient World and the Origins of Biblical History* (New Haven: Yale University Press, 1983) 322-37.

book of Joshua, 4QJosh[a], which preserves parts of chs. 5–10, and 4QJosh[b], with portions of chs. 2–4; 17. The latter reflects the same basic text as the MT with a few readings that agree with the LXX or are independent.[6] However, 4QJosh[a] represents a shorter, more original text than either the MT or the LXX. Of particular interest is its placement of the altar-building story at the end of Joshua 8 (MT 8:30-35) or the beginning of ch. 9 (LXX 9:2a-f). The passage has long been recognized by scholars as a problem for three reasons. First, it interrupts the narrative, which most naturally flows from the account of the destruction of Ai ending in 8:29 to that of the reaction of the Gibeonites to the news about Jericho and Ai in 9:3. Second, its setting at Mount Ebal, some 30 miles from Ai and even farther from the Israelite camp at Gilgal, makes no sense. Third, it also makes no sense that the Israelites would wait until after the defeats of Jericho and Ai to build their first altar in the land rather than doing so immediately after crossing into Canaan, especially since this is what Deut 27:5 prescribes.

The reading of 4QJosh[a] avoids the first and third of these difficulties by placing the altar story before ch. 5 and thus immediately after the Jordan crossing, as one would expect. Unfortunately, the text of 4QJosh[a] begins toward the end of 8:34 (MT), after the point at which Ebal and Gerizim are mentioned in the MT and LXX, so it is impossible to tell whether it located the event at Mounts Ebal and Gerizim as do the MT and LXX. Given this placement of the story, however, it seems likely that 4QJosh[a] did not locate the altar building at Mount Ebal. The MT and LXX reflect misplacement of the episode after the identification of its setting with Mount Ebal in Deut 27:4.[7] In other words, 4QJosh[a] reflects yet a third version of Joshua — an older and better one than the MT and LXX — and it suggests that at least some of the problems presented by the book may have occurred quite late in its development and are due to its preservation in different versions. Unfortunately, 4QJosh[a] is too fragmentary to offer much more than tantalizing possibilities when it comes to the other issues raised about the book's compositional history.

---

6. See Emanuel Tov, "4QJosh[b]," in *Qumran Cave 4.IX*, ed. Eugene C. Ulrich, Frank Moore Cross, et al. *DJD* 14 (1995) 153-60.

7. Eugene Ulrich, "4QJosh[a]," in Ulrich and Cross, *DJD* 14 (1995) 143-52. As Ulrich observes, the identification in Deuteronomy was probably made in reaction to the Samaritan claims about Mount Gerizim as a sacred site.

History and Archaeology

The book of Joshua presents readers with a particular portrait of Israel's emergence as a nation in the land of Canaan. This portrait, as we have seen, corresponds to the book's two halves and can be summarized in the following terms: invasion and conquest, division and settlement. Nevertheless, tensions between the two halves, which we have also observed, already suggest that this portrait is an idealized one at best, and these tensions will be exacerbated by Judges and later books that indicate a substantial Canaanite presence in the land following Joshua's conquests. Not surprisingly, therefore, the actual historical process behind Israel's emergence as indicated by archaeological evidence appears to have been much more complex than the portrait in Joshua.

Since archaeology has played a significant role in evaluating the historical validity of the conquest story in Joshua, it is crucial to have some sense of how archaeology works. First of all, archaeologists divide ancient history into broad periods designated according to the primary materials used to make tools and weapons as humans evolved culturally. The two broad periods that are relevant here are the Bronze Age (ca. 3200-1200 B.C.E.) and the Iron Age (1200-333). These are subdivided, respectively, into the Early (3200-2000), Middle (2000-1550), and Late (1550-1200) Bronze Ages and the Iron I (1200-1000) and Iron II (1000-333) periods. The dates are approximate, and the transitions from one period to another should be thought of as gradual rather than instant.

Despite some efforts to place the conquest described in Joshua in the Middle Bronze Age, mainly to accommodate the story of Jericho's fall, biblical scholars and archaeologists generally agree that the setting envisioned for the story is the Late Bronze Age and the transition from Bronze to Iron. In broader historical perspective, this period witnessed the presence of local city-states ruled by petty dynasties in Canaan and the decline of Egyptian hegemony controlling them, as well as the invasion of the Sea Peoples from the western Mediterranean, the best known of whom were the Philistines. Israel, or part of it, may have been among a group of people whose designation in Egyptian inscriptions as the ʿApiru or Habiru is tantalizingly similar, but not an exact match, to the name "Hebrew." However, the ʿApiru/Habiru were a social class of mercenaries and brigands living on the fringes of settled society rather than an ethnic group.

Two further characteristics of archaeology, especially as it relates to the Bible, merit some discussion. First, archaeology cannot prove the Bible. If, for example, the book of Joshua claims that the Israelites under Joshua conquered and destroyed a specific Canaanite city and archaeological excavation confirms the city's destruction in the Late Bronze period, archaeology still has not proven the historical validity of the Bible's account. This is because archaeology does not usually explain cause and certainly not ultimate cause. The destruction layer shows that the city burned at a particular point in time, but it does not demonstrate whether the burning was accidental or intentional and, if the latter, whether the attackers were Israelites, Egyptians, or other Canaanites, much less whether it was ultimately God who brought about the defeat.

In a sense, the reverse principle — that archaeology cannot disprove the Bible — is also true. If the city in question shows no evidence of destruction, then archaeology may have proven the unreliability of the Bible's details for historical reconstruction. But the purpose of the Bible's account may not be historical in a modern, journalistic sense. Rather, its purpose may be etiological — showing that what was once a Canaanite city became Israelite. In this respect, archaeology succeeds in showing only that the Bible should not be read as a modern historiographical document. Where archaeology is most helpful to the study of the Bible is not in efforts to prove or disprove but in providing background and context to the world and culture assumed by the biblical writers and their audiences. A particular branch of archaeology, ethnoarchaeology, is especially important for the parallels it provides from other societies for cultural phenomena depicted in the Bible, such as ethnic identity, the transition from one culture or ethnic group to another, and the evolution within a society from tribal organization to national state and monarchy.

The second characteristic of archaeology that should be highlighted is that it requires interpretation. This runs counter to the widespread idea that the Bible has to be interpreted but archaeology is scientific fact. In fact, interpretation is involved at every level of archaeological work. To begin with, there is the matter of site identification. The identification of a ruined city with one mentioned in the Bible is usually a matter of interpretation, since it is rare that such an archaeological site yields any self-identification. The city of Gibeon, which plays a role in Joshua, is that rare exception. However, archaeologists typically identify biblical cities based on geographical descriptions in the Bible and other ancient documents as well as modern Arabic names, which often preserve the ancient designations. Again, el-Jib, the modern name for the site of Gibeon, is a good example.

In addition to site identification, dating is also a matter of interpretation. How does an archaeologist know whether the destruction layer at a site is from the presumed time of Joshua (Late Bronze Age) or from, say, three centuries earlier in the Middle Bronze period? The answer is pottery, specifically the charted typological development of techniques of pottery manufacture, style, and decoration. But while there is widespread agreement among archaeologists about the general contours of ceramic typology and the hallmark features of certain periods, there is also plenty of room for differences in interpretation when it comes to applying these criteria to specific finds.

Turning now to the book of Joshua for the specific application of these observations about archaeology and history, we may note that the story of the conquest in Joshua is part of a larger issue regarding Israel's origin that involves the exodus story and even, to some extent, the traditions about the patriarchs. The fact is that we do not know exactly where Israel came from. The oldest inscription bearing the name "Israel" was left on a stela by Pharaoh Merneptah ca. 1207 B.C.E. The inscription reads, "Israel is laid waste; its seed is no more." This statement is an exaggeration for propaganda purposes. Still, it is difficult, if not impossible, to align the Israel of the Merneptah stela with that of the Bible. For one thing, the date of the Merneptah stela does not accord well the Bible's chronology, and vice-versa. For example, if Ramesses the Great was the pharaoh of the oppression of the Hebrews, as implied by the place names in Exod 1:11, then Merneptah, his son, would be the pharaoh of the exodus (Exod 2:23). But the stela mentions Israel already in the land of Canaan in Merneptah's fifth year and therefore does not allow for a forty-year wilderness wandering. To complicate matters further, the chronological problem is just one facet of the much larger difficulty that there is simply no real evidence that the exodus ever occurred at all. There is no reference in all of the vast literature from ancient Egypt to the exodus or any of the events or persons associated with it, nor is there any archaeological evidence to support its historicity.

The conquest narrative in Joshua 1–11 suffers from almost the same total absence of evidence. It focuses on four cities: Jericho (chs. 2–6), Ai (chs. 7–8), Gibeon (9:1–10:15), and Hazor (11:1-11). Succinctly, the archaeological evidence regarding each of these places is as follows. The best archaeological work indicates that Jericho's famous walls were finally destroyed at the end of the Middle Bronze Age, around 1550 B.C.E., and that in the thirteenth century, when the Israelites purportedly arrived, an unwalled village stood on a portion of its ruins. Ai's destruction occurred even earlier, in the Early Bronze Age, about 2400, or some one thousand years or more before the Israelites. Similar to Jericho, Gibeon shows occupation in the Early and Middle Bronze periods and then again in the Iron Age, but virtually none during the Late Bronze. Hazor alone of the four attests destruction during the thirteenth century, though the agent of the destruction is uncertain. Essentially the same situation pertains to the cities in the summary list in Josh 12:9-24. The location of some of these is uncertain (Debir, Makkedah, Libnah, Eglon). But among those that can be identified, only a few (Hazor, Lachish, Megiddo) attest destruction in the thirteenth century, though it remains uncertain by whom. Most show no such destruction, either because they were unoccupied at the time (Jericho, Ai, Arad) or because they were continuously occupied with no change of population apparent in the archaeological record (Jerusalem, Hebron, Gezer). Jerusalem, for instance, is occupied by Jebusites and not conquered by Israel until David two centuries later according to 2 Sam 5:6-10. In short, present-day archaeology offers no clear evidence in support of the invasion and conquest model as an explanation of Israel's origins. What clear evidence it does offer, in fact, suggests that there was no such conquest.

This has led scholars to propose alternative models. The two best known of these are typically dubbed the "infiltration" and "peasant revolt" models. The former is associated with the great German scholars Albrecht Alt and Martin Noth. They believed that Israel did indeed enter Canaan from the outside, but that instead of taking over by means of military conquest the Israelites gained dominance gradually. Also, while there were occasional skirmishes, this was a mostly peaceful process. The "peasant revolt" or "social revolution" model, suggested by George Mendenhall and elaborated by Norman Gottwald, held that Israel did not enter Canaan from the outside but was a population indigenous to the land. Its ascendancy came about through socioeconomic and political struggle against the upper-class Canaanite city-states. The struggle was aided ideologically by devotion to Yahweh.

The most recent, cutting-edge archaeological research has tended to support the notion of social revolution in some form. This research has focused on an emergent culture appearing in small, unwalled settlements in the central highlands of Canaan at the threshhold of the Late Bronze/Early

Iron Ages. The material culture (pottery and the like) and inscriptional remains of this culture are continuous with Late Bronze Age Canaanite forms, but the highland settlements lay outside the control of the Canaanite city-states. In other words, the initial element of Israel appears to have been Canaanite in culture and ethnicity. What distinguished Israel from its Canaanite origins was not ethnic identity but social structure. The absence of larger "elitist" buildings in the architecture has been interpreted as indicating that the society of these villages was egalitarian rather than hierarchical. A tiered social structure consisting of individual, extended family, clan, and tribe is reflected in certain biblical stories (Joshua 7; 1 Samuel 10). What united the different families into clans and then tribes may have been the advent of new technologies, such as terracing and lined cisterns, that permitted the cultivation of the highland terrain in cooperation with other clans and tribes. The union of the tribes into a nation was perhaps effected by the need for defense (reflected in 1 Samuel 8; Judges 4) and the worship of Yahweh. The eventual move to monarchy took place not as the importation of a foreign institution, as implied in the Bible (1 Samuel 8), but in a continuum with Canaanite culture.

The riddle of Israel's origin is still not solved by any means. The history and process of the development of Israel match the history and process of the development of the book of Joshua in complexity, and the two are related. It may well be, in fact, that ancient Israel was something of a "melting pot" with citizens who had different origins — some from outside of Canaan, some with indigenous roots. As a result, there are remnants of different origin traditions preserved in the Bible. Even within the book of Joshua, there is acknowledgement of some indigenous Canaanite elements (Rahab's family, the Gibeonites) incorporated within Israel.

The major conquest stories, however, are probably best explained etiologically and theologically. The name "Ai" means ruin, and the story of its conquest showed how it became so. Jericho also lay in ruins at the purported time of Joshua, yet its once magnificent walls symbolized Canaanite culture at what must have been its apex. The story of its conquest, in which cultic ritual is key, shows how Yahweh gave the city over to Israel. The point is that the land is Yahweh's to give and that proper service to Yahweh is essential for Israel to receive and maintain the gift.

Before leaving the topic of the historical validity of the book of Joshua, we should say something about the man himself. Was Joshua a historical personage? Scholars have pointed to a number of curious features relative to Joshua in the Hebrew Bible and especially his namesake book that sharpen this question. Joshua appears in two basic roles in the Bible: as Moses' helper and successor, who led the conquest of Canaan, and as one of the spies who, along with Caleb, brought back a favorable report (Numbers 13–14). However, some suspect that his presence as a faithful spy may be secondary in the tradition, since Caleb appears alone in some contexts (Num 13:30-31; Deut 1:36-38) and since Joshua is identified as originally named Hoshea (Num 13:8, 16). This Joshua is from the tribe of Ephraim, instead of Benjamin, where most of the conquest stories in Joshua 1–12 are set. This has led to the suggestion that he was originally at home in the stories about the northern conquest in Joshua 10–11 and only secondarily became associated with the traditions about the conquest as a whole in chs. 1–12. His role in these chapters mirrors Moses in quite a few respects: both divide bodies of water, Moses the Re(e)d Sea, Joshua the Jordan; both have an encounter with the divine, Moses at the burning bush, Joshua with the commander of Yahweh's army; both inscribe laws on stone (Josh 8:32; 24:26); both allot land, Moses east of the Jordan, Joshua west. In short, the depiction of Joshua in the book of Joshua seems to be, at least in some measure, a traditional or literary imitation of Moses. Finally, there is the name Joshua itself, which means "Yahweh saves" or "gives victory" — certainly an appropriate name for the role of the figure of Joshua in the Bible and perhaps more than simple coincidence.

Themes and Ideology

The book of Joshua is rich in religious and political themes that might have spoken in different ways to readers at different stages of its composition. Among the major themes of the book, we can highlight the following four: land, obedience, leadership, and victory. These themes are tightly interlaced, and their interrelationship is part of the book's sophistication and message. Hence, rather than treating them independently, it is preferable to describe their working together as a whole.

The land of Canaan is Yahweh's gift to his people in fulfillment of the promises made to their ancestors. It is spoken of in Joshua as Israel's "heritage" or "inheritance" from Yahweh. The conquest is a religious experience, involving cultic processions and the proper observance of rituals such as circumcision and the Passover. Jericho's conquest is effected through liturgical, not military, means, and it is Yahweh who makes its walls collapse. Achan's religious offense results in defeat and must be made right before the conquest can continue. Then the land is divided by lot, i.e., according to divine will. The land as a whole is crucial to Israel's identity as a nation, and each tribe's allotment is crucial to its identity within the nation.

The land is a tangible sign of Yahweh's faithfulness and of Israel's obedience to Yahweh. The conquest and retention of the land are dependent on obedience, a theme that plays large in the DtrH. The tension that the book of Joshua presents between complete and incomplete conquest, then, reflects Israel's history of struggle with obedience and disobedience and its consequent hold on and loss of the land at different periods. At one level, the complete conquest of the land and the boundaries both of the whole and of individual tribes may be idealized — a utopian vision of what Israel can be if it will obey. The same may be said for the depiction of the non-Israelite kings and people cowering in fear before Israel. This depiction may have provided comfort in the face of the constant threat and experience of foreign domination that was Israel's usual fare. This reality is reflected in another, less optimistic level or facet of the book — that in which so much of the land remains unconquered as a result of Israel's unfaithfulness.

A significant part of Israel's success in the conquest is due to faithful leadership. Joshua is a worthy successor to Moses, whose work he duplicates in several particulars. Some scholars have also seen Joshua as a royal figure in anticipation above all of the seventh-century King Josiah of Judah, who is a leading hero of the DtrH. Thus, an integral part of the portrait of conquest in Joshua is the model of leadership that it furnishes as a crucial element in the retention of the land.

The land is Yahweh's to bestow upon Israel because it belongs to him. As Deuteronomy 32 points out, Israel — people and land — is Yahweh's own allotment and heritage. It is in this context that one of the most difficult themes for modern readers — that of "holy war" — must be understood. Since the land is Yahweh's property, it is in a sense sacred. This is why it is conquered through ritual and retained by faithful obedience. As the owner of the land, Yahweh decides who lives on it. It is Yahweh, as the Divine Warrior, who fights on Israel's behalf and whose victory brings "rest" from war to both people and land. Those who encroach on divine property are to be sacrificed — hence, the order to carry out *ḥerem* — the annihilation of everything that breathes. The "holy war" motif has a long, distasteful history of (mis)interpretation, the danger of which is perhaps clearest in the horrific treatment of the indigenous Native Americans by European Christians who saw themselves in the role of the chosen people taking over the promised land. It may bring some relief to modern readers scandalized by the occurrence of this genocidal theme in the Bible to realize that it was probably never really carried out under Joshua. Like the boundaries of the land, it was a piece of an idealized vision by people who were usually at the mercy of foreign invaders. Moreover, at the time Joshua was written, the Canaanites, from whom the Israelites themselves likely originated, had long since disappeared, if they even ever existed as such an identifiable ethnic group.

Reading Strategies

Three concrete strategies may be useful to readers approaching the book of Joshua. First, consult a map as you read. There is no need to chart the boundaries in the lists in the second half of the book. There are maps with those boundaries already drawn, to the extent that they can be reconstructed. (Some of the place names are unknown.) Besides, most people will probably skip those chapters anyway. But a map is indispensable for understanding the geographic movement of the narrative in Joshua. It also makes clear the confines of the area that is the focus of chs. 2–9 and the extent to which Shechem and Mounts Ebal and Gerizim lie outside of that area. A map shows the proximity of Ai to Bethel and thus helps one to understand why some scholars have proposed that Ai was mistaken for Bethel in the story of its destruction.

A second suggested strategy is to pay close attention to the genre of the material one is reading. Aside from the boundary lists, there are only two basic genres in the book — narrative and speech. It is important to recognize the point of view from which the narratives and speeches are recounted and to raise critical questions about it. How, for instance, does Rahab know about the Re(e)d Sea and Sihon and Og? On the one hand, her expressed knowledge of such Israelite, indeed Dtr traditions, is a patent indication that the speech is a composition of the Israelite author rather than a transcription by the Israelite spies. On the other hand, the characterization of Rahab — a Canaanite woman! — as well informed, clever, and a skilled negotiator is remarkable and may reflect an author's subtle way of undermining the larger text's advocacy of ethnic genocide in favor of a more universalistic perspective.

Along similar lines, a third and final strategy is to read carefully with an awareness of the tensions in the book that are reflective of differing perspectives. Does a particular text present the conquest as complete or incomplete? At the same time, it is worthwhile to keep in mind the question of the book's unitary message. Does it, in fact, have a single or overall message to convey? If so, how does one account for the apparent contradictions? Are there elements of the book that make use of irony or sarcasm? How would ancient readers at different periods have understood the book's message in their different contexts? These questions are sharpened by consideration of the fact that the book of Joshua is one piece in an even larger unit, the DtrH.

5

Judges

Moses is dead. Joshua is dead. There is no king yet in Israel. The book of
Judges is about the period between the conquest and the monarchy, when
Israel was led by charismatic military figures known as "judges." The book
begins essentially where Joshua ended, by mentioning Joshua's death (Judg
1:1). It also picks up the topic of the incomplete conquest. If that topic is
downplayed in Joshua, it is foremost at the beginning of Judges, where the
Israelites raise the question of who — that is, which tribe — should go first
to fight against the Canaanites and take possession of its allotment. The
fact that the question is raised directly of Yahweh highlights Israel's leaderless status, as does the book's concluding observation that at that time
there was no king in Israel (21:25).

Content and Structure

Three large sections of the book of Judges can be readily distinguished
based on content:

> Introductory material (1:1–3:6)
> Stories and information about the judges (3:7–16:31)
> Concluding stories (chs. 17–21)

Each of these sections can be subdivided. There are, for instance, two introductions to the book (1:1–2:5; 2:6–3:6), based on separate references to

Joshua's death in 1:1 and 2:8. Then, the middle section combines stories about military deliverers (3:7–9:57; 10:6–12:7) with lists of civil functionaries (10:1-5; 12:8-15), and each judge has an account devoted to him or her. Finally, there are also two distinct stories unrelated to judges that conclude the book (chs. 17–18; 19–21). A detailed outline of the book looks like this:

Introductory material (1:1–3:6)
First introduction: Successes and failures to conquer the land (1:1–2:5)
Second introduction: Apostasy and the pattern of the judges (2:6–3:6)
Stories and information about the judges (3:7–16:31)
Military deliverers (3:7–9:37)
    Othniel (3:7-11)
    Ehud (3:12-30)
    Shamgar (3:31)
    Deborah (chs. 4–5)
    Gideon (chs. 6–8)
    Abimelech (ch. 9)
Civil functionaries (10:1–12:15)
    Tola (10:1-2)
    Jair (10:3-5)
Jephthah (10:6–12:7)
    Ibzan (12:8-10)
    Elon (12:11-12)
    Abdon (12:13-15)
Samson (chs. 13–16)
Concluding stories (chs. 17–21)
First conclusion: Micah and the Danites (chs. 17–18)
    Micah the Ephraimite builds a shrine and acquires a Levite (ch. 17)
    The Danites move and take Micah's shrine and priest (ch. 18)
Second conclusion: Outrage and civil war (chs. 19–21)
    The Levite and his concubine attacked in Gibeah (ch. 19)
    War with Benjamin (ch. 20)
    Wives for the Benjaminites (ch. 21)

Title

The title "Judges" derives from the LXX by way of the Latin Vulgate and is based on the title used in the description of the office in 2:16-19. Outside of this passage, the noun form occurs in the book only in 11:27, where it refers to Yahweh rather than a human. The verb form occurs throughout the book. The Semitic root from which both noun and verb come (*špṭ*) can have nuances relating to ruling and leading in battle, which are certainly appropriate for the role of the protagonists in the book. However, it seems likely, as Martin Noth surmised, that the term originated in the list of civil functionaries (10:1-5; 12:8-5) and was applied by the Dtr author to the deliverers, especially since the references to the latter judging Israel are in the Dtr frames around their stories (see below on composition).

Composition

As with Joshua, as well as subsequent books in the DtrH, it is perhaps most helpful to conceive of the book of Judges developing in three stages: pre-Dtr sources, Dtr composition, and post-Dtr additions.

Pre-Dtr Sources

It seems evident from the above overview and outline of contents that Dtr's sources for the book were of two basic types — stories about military deliverers and a list of civil functionaries. The reasons for seeing them as two distinct types become clearer when the information about them is laid out in table form. The military deliverers include Othniel, Ehud, Deborah, Gideon, Jephthah, and Samson. The pertinent details drawn from the tales about them are their tribes, enemies, length of oppression before their deliverance, and length of the period of "rest" for the land.

The table on page 60 does not include either Shamgar (3:31) or Abimelech (Judges 9), both of which were later additions to the tales of the judges (see below). It is uncertain whether these tales came to Dtr in oral or written form. Scholars also debate whether Dtr received the stories independently or already as a collection, though the former position seems more likely in view of the changes that can be ascribed to Dtr (see below).

Military Deliverers

Judge	Tribe	Enemy	Years of oppression	Years of rest
Othniel	Judah	Cushan-rishathaim Aram-naharaim	8	40
Ehud	Benjamin	Eglon of Moab	18	80
Deborah	Ephraim	Jabin of Canaan, Sisera his general	20	40
Gideon	Manasseh	Midian	7	40
Jephthah	Gilead	Philistines & Ammonites	18	6
Samson	Dan	Philistines	40	20

The different tribal origins and different enemies are indications that the judges may have been local heroes and contemporaries rather than operating sequentially on a national stage. The figures for the years of oppression seem realistic and not artificial, with the exception of the one for the Philistine domination leading to Samson. On the other hand, the figures for the years of rest are all round numbers — 40, twice 40 (Ehud), or half 40 (Samson) — with 40 years representing the length of a generation. The only exception here is Jephthah, whose tenure of six years as judge fits better with the civil functionaries, as we will see shortly.

Within the pre-Dtr stories of deliverers themselves there are signs of literary development. A good example is the story of Deborah, which is told in prose (ch. 4) and poetic (ch. 5) forms. The two differ significantly, the major difference between them being the way in which Jael kills Sisera.[1] In the prose, he is lying asleep in her tent, when she drives a tent peg through his skull (4:21), while in the poem, he is standing and she smashes his skull with a notorious "blunt instrument" (5:26-27). The difference probably stems from the prose writer's interpretation of the poem's reference to the hammer and tent peg (5:26) as two separate implements. In actuality, this is an example of poetic parallelism in which similar ideas are expressed in dif-

---

1. The following treatment is based on Baruch Halpern, *The First Historians: The Hebrew Bible and History* (San Francisco: Harper & Row, 1988) 76-97.

ferent ways in two lines of poetry. It is a common technique of Hebrew poetry, perhaps even its hallmark characteristic. For instance, earlier in the poem it reads, "Yahweh, when you went out from Seir/When you marched from the region of Edom" (5:4). Here it is obvious that "went out" = "marched," and Seir = the region of Edom. Similarly, later in 5:28, when the mother of Sisera asks, "Why is his chariot so long in coming?/Why tarry the hoofbeats of his chariots?" she is referring in two ways to the same event, namely, her son's return from battle. In the same way, 5:26 uses two parallel lines to refer to the same thing. That is, Jael grasps a single implement, not two. As is clear from the rest of the verse, Jael uses this implement to strike Sisera a fatal blow. The exact nature of the implement is unimportant, except that it is some item associated with erecting a tent, since Jael is a tent-dweller. The language about Sisera sinking and falling in v. 27 also makes clear that he is envisioned as standing when she struck him.

The author of the prose has interpreted Jael's act in 5:26 as two separate actions involving two different implements in order to present a more creative account of Sisera's death. Thus, Jael takes both a tent peg and a hammer, in separate hands, and then nails his head to her floor (4:21). This interpretation, in turn, led to other details in the prose account. In order for her to drive the peg through his skull, he needed to be lying down asleep and thus inside of the tent. Jael brought him in under the pretense of giving him drink and hiding him, which is why she covered him. This required his pursuers to be relatively close behind him, which in turn required that he be on foot (4:17), despite the indications of the poem that he drove a chariot. The dependence of the prose version on the poem accords with the widely held view that the poem is one of the oldest pieces of literature in the Hebrew Bible. It may have come in oral or in written form to the prose author, who creatively rewrote it to produce the version in Judges 4.

The other major source used by Dtr in the composition of Judges was the list of civil functionaries, which included Tola, Jair, Jephthah, Ibzan, Elon, and Abdon. While it is not certain whether the stories of deliverers came to Dtr individually or already as a collection, the civil functionaries were almost certainly a list. The material about the functionaries does not consist of stories, but only brief notices about their family members and the like. They are not military deliverers. They have no enemy associated with them and nothing about years of oppression. There is also, therefore, no language about the land having rest following their victory. Rather, they are simply said to have judged Israel for a period of time.

Civil Functionaries

Judge	Tribe	Length of judgeship
Tola	Issachar/Ephraim	23
Jair	Gilead	22
Jephthah	Gilead	6
Ibzan	Judah	7
Elon	Ephraim	8
Abdon	Zebulun	10

Jephthah's presence in both sources — among the deliverers and in the list of civil functionaries — is indicated by the fact that the material about him shares features with the other entries in both sources. Thus, there is a story about Jephthah's military deliverance of Israel, in common with the "major" judges, but the story stands in the middle of the list of functionaries. Also, the figure for the length of his judgeship is not a round multiple of forty, as is typical for the deliverers, but the specific number, six. And the text refers to the number of years he judged Israel, as it does for the other "minor" judges, rather than the length of the land's rest, as is typical for the deliverers.

Dtr's Composition

It was Dtr who combined these two sources or kinds of sources and gave the book of Judges its basic shape. There are good traces in the narrative of Dtr's compositional activities, and we may sketch the steps he took as follows. To begin with, the second introduction in 2:6–3:6 was actually the first one written, as it was composed by Dtr following up on Joshua's speech in Joshua 23. In this introduction, especially 2:16-19, Dtr laid out the basic pattern for his account of each of the military deliverers, which consists of the following stages:

Israel sins by worshipping other gods
Yahweh sends a foreign power that oppresses the Israelites for a period of years
Yahweh, moved to pity by Israel's suffering and outcry, sends a judge

The judge rescues Israel by defeating the oppressor and bringing
"rest" to the land

After the judge's death, Israel sins, thus beginning the cycle again

Dtr used the first judge, Othniel, as a paradigm for this pattern, even filling
it out with some additional elements. The Israelites do evil by worshipping
other gods (3:7), so an angry Yahweh sends King Cushan-rishathaim of
Aram-naharaim to oppress Israel for eight years (3:8). But when the Israelites cry out, Yahweh raises up a deliverer in the person of Othniel (3:9),
who is impelled by Yahweh's spirit to lead Israel to war (3:10) and serves as
a judge for forty years after the victory. It is impossible to know how much
of the information in this passage, if any, is from source material. It is thoroughly Deuteronomistic in its language and orientation. There are few details, and those that are present show signs of manipulation. For instance,
the name "Cushan-rishathaim" means something like "dark, double
wicked" and may be an invention, though perhaps based on a real name.
Aram-naharaim (= "Aram between the two rivers"), which is upper Mesopotamia, east of Syria, might have been chosen for its rhyme with Cushan-
rishathaim. The name Othniel and the figure of eight years for the length
of oppression seem unlikely to have been inventions and may have some
origin in tradition. However, the forty-year tenure of Othniel employs a
round number for a generation that is common in the Dtr accounts of the
"major" judges, as we have seen.

Having composed the account of Othniel's judgeship as a model, Dtr
arranged the military deliverers sequentially. As we saw above, the tales
that Dtr inherited were traditions about local heroes from different tribes
who were probably contemporaries. Dtr enclosed his account of each
judge within a framework that applied his cyclical pattern to that judge,
i.e., detailing the renewed apostasy of Israel, the identity of the oppressor
and years of oppression, the crying out of Israel in oppression, and, following the story of the judge's victory, the length of the judge's tenure during
which the land had rest. The application of this theological pattern turned
the local heroes into national leaders who followed one after the other. Dtr
filled out this sequence with a chronological scheme based on forty years
for a generation. From Othniel of Judah as the first judge, Dtr further arranged the other deliverers such that their tribal origins proceeded in geographical order from south to north, starting with Judah and ending with
Dan, if Samson is included, or with Gilead east of the Jordan, if Jephthah

was the last of Dtr's deliverers. In short, Dtr's theological pattern involved political, chronological, and geographical dimensions.

Compared to the deliverers, the civil functionaries played a minor role in Dtr's arrangement of the book. The presence of Jephthah's name among both was probably the key factor that led Dtr to combine them as he did, recounting the stories of the deliverers up to Jephthah and then affixing the list of civil functionaries, telling the story of Jephthah in conjunction with his place in that list, which may have been at its end. Dtr then borrowed the title of the civil functionaries — "judge" — and applied it to the military deliverers as well. Thus, while the contribution of the functionaries in the book was small in volume, it was great in terms of nomenclature.

Post-Dtr Additions

Several passages in Judges show signs of being post-Dtr additions. The first introduction (1:1–2:5) is in obvious tension with the Dtr introduction (2:6–3:6) in presuming Joshua's death (1:1). It thus seems connected with the second address of Joshua (ch. 24) concluding that book. This is not to claim that all of 1:1–2:5 is of a piece, since 2:1-5 offers a different explanation for the indigenous people being left in the land than the material either before or after it. Judges 1 rather straightforwardly reports the successes and failures of the different Israelite tribes in taking the land. Dtr's explanation (2:22) is that those who remained were left by Yahweh as a test. But in 2:3, they are a punishment for unfaithfulness and a snare. The additions may have occurred in both cases after the DtrH was divided into discrete books, coordinating the end of Joshua with its namesake's death.

Along similar lines, the concluding two stories in chs. 17–21 have nothing to do with judges or external enemies. Instead, the final story details a civil war. These stories do not presuppose Israel's conflict with the Philistines as oppressors and therefore interrupt the continuity between Judges (13:1) and 1 Samuel (1 Sam 7:13) in this regard. Rather, the purpose of these tales seems to be to illustrate religious and social decay pointing to the need for a king (Judg 17:6; 18:1; 19:1), which is the theme on which the book ends (21:25). It may be that the failures at complete conquest in the first introduction were meant to point to this need as well. The clause in 18:30, "until the land went into captivity," most naturally alludes to the fall of the northern kingdom in 721 B.C.E. and suggests that the stories in Judges 17–21 arose long after the purported period of the judges. Like the first introduction, the concluding stories in these chapters were probably added after the separation of the DtrH into distinct books.

Other post-Dtr additions pertain to the major judges. Judges 3:31 devotes one verse between the tales of Ehud and Deborah to Shamgar. Shamgar is unique because there is no notice of sin or oppression connected with him and no figures for the length of oppression or rest, as there are for all the other deliverers. Furthermore, the mention of Israel sinning after Ehud in 4:1 indicates no awareness of Shamgar in the Dtr version of the book. The reason for Shamgar's addition at this point was evidently to anticipate the mention of him in the old poem known as the Song of Deborah in Judges 5 (v. 6).

Another possible addition to Dtr's version of Judges is the story of Abimelech in ch. 9, which was appended to the Gideon story by way of the identification of Abimelech's father, Jerubbaal, with Gideon (6:32; 7:1; 8:35). However, the story is quite unlike those of the judges. Abimelech is not a judge at all and is never called one. To the contrary, he tries to make himself king. The disaster that ensues no doubt has something to do with the reason the story was included — perhaps as an indictment of kingship as an institution.

Finally, the Samson stories may also have been added to Judges, though there is considerable uncertainty among scholars on this point. It is true that in some ways the story of Samson fits with those of the other deliverers. Israel sins yet again, and Yahweh sends an oppressor, the Philistines. There are figures for the length of oppression (forty years) and of Samson's tenure as judge (twenty years). But in many other ways, the stories about Samson differ from those of other judges, and he does not fit the profile. For instance, he never completely succeeds in delivering Israel from the Philistines. In fact, most of his activities have to do with personal vengeance revolving around his affairs with Philistine women rather than a spirit-driven effort to rescue Israel. Less dramatic is the figure for the length of oppression leading to Samson (forty years), which appears artificial in contrast to the realistic numbers for the other deliverers. The Samson material itself may be layered or a collection of once independent tales. The summary of Samson's judgeship (15:20; 16:31) suggests that ch. 16 is an interpolation. Also, chs. 14–15 do not mention the Nazirite vow or Samson's long hair, but seem to attribute Samson's strength to the onrush of

Yahweh's spirit (14:19; 15:14), while the vow and his hair are focus points of the stories in chs. 13 and 16.

Text

The oldest variant textual witnesses are not as well represented for Judges as they are for other books like Joshua and Samuel. The manuscripts of the LXX reflect early revision toward the MT and therefore do not represent the original Greek translation known as the Old Greek. There were fragments of three scrolls found among the Dead Sea Scrolls, one from Cave 1 (1QJudg) and two from Cave 4 (4QJudg^a and 4QJudg^b). All three are sparsely represented — 4QJudg^a by a single fragment and 4QJudg^b by three fragments from Judges 19 and 21. Nearly two dozen fragments of 1QJudg are extant, but most are so small that their location in the book cannot be identified. Those that can be located (nine) are from chs. 6, perhaps 8, and 9.

Despite this paucity of evidence, the fragments hint at the same kind of textual diversity as is more evident for other books. While 1QJudg and 4QJudg^b both appear to be close to the MT, the 4QJudg^a fragment contains readings unrelated to other extant witnesses. Of particular note is the fact that the fragment, which encompasses Judg 6:2-13, lacks vv. 7-10, a text that scholars have long suspected of being a late intrusion because it interrupts the narrative and is so different from its surrounding context. This suggests that 4QJudg^a preserves an earlier version of the book of Judges than that of the MT. Unfortunately, the single fragment permits only a tantalizing glimpse at this version.

History

From the evidence regarding the composition of the book of Judges, it should be clear that the period of the judges as a time in which Israel *as a nation* was ruled by charismatic military heroes was an invention by Dtr. Israel did not come to exist as a nation until after the advent of the monarchy. On the other hand, the stories of the deliverers inherited by Dtr seem to reflect a social/political setting that basically corresponds with what appears from the archaeological record to be Israel's situation in the Early

Iron Age. At this time, Israel was not yet a nation/state. There was no monarchy or any other centralized government. At most, "Israel" consisted of a loose confederation of tribes and villages located mainly in the central highlands of Palestine. As surmised from a careful analysis of the pre-Dtr stories about the deliverers, they were most likely heroes of individual tribes fighting against localized enemies. This portrait of a rather anarchical situation where distinct tribes and clans in the central highlands fought against city-state kings does fit in broad terms with the model of Israel's emergence as a rural, "egalitarian" society in the central highlands of Canaan described above in Chapter Four.

The Song of Deborah in Judges 5 is again of particular interest for the historical situation, both for what it says and for what it does not say. The song is a celebration of victory on the part of a confederation of Israelite tribes or clans against a coalition of Canaanite kings. What is interesting, however, is the tribes that are mentioned by name (and those that are omitted) and the roles they play. The tribes that are praised for answering Deborah's call and going to war are Ephraim, Benjamin, Machir, Zebulun, Issachar, and Naphtali (5:14-15a, 18) — all tribes located in the northern central highlands. There is, however, no tribe of Machir in lists of the "standard" twelve tribes. Machir is listed elsewhere as a "son" or subclan of Manasseh (Gen 50:23; Num 26:29; Josh 13:31). It may have been an independent clan that was eventually absorbed within Manasseh. At any rate, it appears here instead of Manasseh, which replaces Machir in later lists. The tribes of Reuben, Gilead, Dan, and Asher do not join the conflict (5:15b-17). Gilead was a subclan or rival of Gad in the same way that Machir was of Manasseh. The southern tribes of Judah and Simeon are not named, nor is the priestly tribe of Levi.

The Song of Deborah, then, seems to reflect a time before Israel could be thought of as a nation, in fact before its makeup was even fixed. What would later become Israel was at this time a group of independent entities — tribes or clans — that apparently felt some affinity with one another, whether because of kinship ties, religion, geographical location, social stratum, or other factors. Whatever ties existed between them did not compel them always to join common cause. The names Machir and Gilead indicate that the identity of at least some tribes was still in flux. The absence of the southern tribes and Levi suggests that they were not considered part of the coalition of tribes at this point in time. However, the reason for their exclusion is uncertain. Given the later division between the kingdoms of Israel and Judah, the northern and southern tribes may always have been independent from one another to a lesser or greater degree.

Plot and Themes

Whatever its relationship to history, the book of Judges is a sophisticated piece of literature. In recent years, scholars have cultivated a greater appreciation of the book — and the Bible in general — as literature, especially in its completed form apart from its history of development. Nowhere is this appreciation more pronounced in the study of the Bible than for the book of Judges. In what follows, we will look at two major themes in the plot of Judges as it stands. They are perhaps the two aspects of the book that leave the greatest impression on readers, and both have long been recognized. The second one especially has been explored in great detail in recent scholarship with interesting results.

The first theme has to do with the cyclical nature of story related in Judges. As noted above, for the deliverers there is a recurring pattern of sin, punishment, repentance and a cry for help, and salvation. The fact that the pattern recurs repeatedly is disturbing, because it suggests that Israel does not learn from its past mistakes. Then again, this may be a characteristic not just of Israel but of human beings in general. Indeed, the repetition of this pattern in conjunction with the author's forty-year generational scheme suggests that each generation of people experienced the cycle anew. There are also positive dimensions to this cycle. It illustrates what the author understands to be the correct human response to disaster in the form of defeat and oppression. That response is repentance and calling on God for help. Above all, the cycle attests the faithfulness of God in responding repeatedly to the outcry of his people and rescuing them. In this perspective, disaster is punishment for sin, but at least it is administered by a loving God who seeks repentance and corrective action. As in the case of the book of Joshua, proper leadership is crucial for maintaining the obedience to God and the prosperity that results. Typically in Judges, Israel's period of rest from oppression endures only as long as the judge designated by Yahweh is alive. Without a righteous leader, the Israelites quickly devolve into sin.

The second theme that the book impresses on readers dovetails with the point about the need for proper, righteous leadership. As the book of

Judges

Judges proceeds, leadership in Israel seems to deteriorate in quality, and the situation of the country grows progressively worse. With Othniel, the paradigm example, and Ehud things are fine. Deborah is certainly a capable leader, but Barak refuses to go to war without her. Also, not all of the tribes rally to her call to war. Gideon has to mediate a dispute with the Ephraimites (8:1-3), and then his son Abimelech causes inner turmoil in his effort to promote his own kingship. Jephthah also fights civil war against Ephraim (12:1-6). As for Samson, he is only out for personal revenge. After his death, the country is leaderless and plunges into apostasy and civil war that almost results in the annihilation of the tribe of Benjamin.

Recent treatments of Judges have observed that a kind of barometer of this deterioration on the part of Israel can be traced in the treatment of women in Judges. At the summit is Deborah, a strong and effective leader. Although Deborah herself does not play a particularly large role in the story, her leadership is supported by another strong and resourceful woman, Jael, who finishes off the enemy general even though she is not Israelite. It is also a resourceful woman who rescues the people of her city by killing the royal pretender Abimelech, throwing a millstone — a tool for grinding grain and hence presumably "women's work" — on his head. But women's stories take a dark turn with Jephthah's daughter, who is sacrificed to fulfill what is at best a foolish vow made by her father. Samson's onetime wife is burned to death (15:6), though Delilah fares better. Both of them seem to be disparaged by the writer for their ethnicity (as Philistines) and perhaps for their gender (as sexually promiscuous) as well. Then the treatment of women in Judges reaches its nadir with the last two sets of stories involving them in the book. The Levite's concubine in Judges 19 suffers horrifically as the victim of rape and dismemberment. Four hundred virgins of Jabesh-gilead are kidnapped to be wives of Benjaminite men, and their families are ritually slaughtered (21:8-12). Then, other young women are abducted from a festival at Shiloh for the same purpose (21:19-24). The author of Judges accounts for these acts of violence particularly against women as signs of social chaos and moral collapse attributable to the lack of central monarchic leadership (21:25).

Tips for Reading

It may be that the most helpful tip for the beginning reader of Judges is to enjoy or appreciate the book as one would other pieces of great literature. Such enjoyment has several facets. One of these relates to characterization in the book. Many of the characters in Judges are complex. Figures like Jephthah or Samson, for example, are not simply all good or all bad. In fact, when it comes to evaluating the characters in the book, the author makes very few explicit judgments. The reader is left free, therefore, to come to his or her own conclusions. If Jephthah and Samson are ambiguous characters, what about Jael or Delilah? Both are non-Israelite. From one perspective, Jael is a hero because she betrays the enemy of Israel, while Delilah is a villain because she betrays an Israelite hero. But from another perspective, Jael could be seen as a traitor, since she kills the commander with whom her people, including her own husband, are at peace, while Delilah might be viewed as a hero to her own people, since she acts to save them against the enemy who had wrought so much destruction among them.

The cases of Jael vs. Sisera and Delilah vs. Samson highlight the sort of "battle of the sexes" that runs as a theme or motif in Judges and that readers may do well to observe. In these two stories, and perhaps in others, there is a good deal of sexual play and innuendo. The tent peg Jael uses to kill Sisera may be seen as a phallic symbol and the penetration of his skull with it as having sexual overtones. There is plenty of imagery and language in the story that can be interpreted sexually and that is used that way elsewhere. For example, Sisera entered Jael's tent; he "lay" down; he was at her feet (5:27; lit., "between her legs"). Even Sisera's mother comforts herself at his delay in the thought that he is enjoying himself with the women (5:30; lit. "wombs") captured as spoil. Samson's encounters with Delilah are not as specific, though he does have his head in her lap (16:19). The scenes between them are also filled with teasing, pouting, and other forms of sexual play and tension. There is no overt description of sexual relations in either story, but the allusions and innuendo are a feature of the artistry with which the book of Judges is narrated.

The reader of Judges might also be struck by the humor in the book. Samson is something of a ridiculous character, whose destruction is really the result of his total lack of restraint, especially where Philistine women are concerned. His poetic verses have a tinge of sarcasm, especially the one in 14:18: "If you had not plowed with my heifer, you would not have found out my riddle." The Ehud story might also raise a chuckle among ancient Israelites. Their enemy, King Eglon, is so fat that Ehud loses his sword when he stabs him in the belly. The king's death goes undetected by his palace servants because the odor of the spilled contents of his colon leads them to believe that he is going about his usual "business" in the bathroom, until he delays so long that it shames them into checking on him (3:24-25). Jotham's parable characterizing Abimelech as a thornbush chosen to be king of the trees because of his uselessness otherwise is a masterpiece of wry sarcasm (9:8-15). The story of Abimelech's death is fully ironic. Its very existence completely undermines Abimelech's desperate attempt to squelch the truth about his death at a woman's hand (9:54).

On a more serious note, the book of Judges is wide open for interpretation on the role and nature of God in the stories it narrates. Some have noticed that God seems less and less involved the further the narrative proceeds, to the point that God is nearly absent from the final stories in the book (chs. 17–21). But then, what is one to make of the Levite's inquiry of God and assurance of the Danites that Yahweh would bless their mission (18:5-6)? The question of God's involvement is even more pressing in other stories. Would God really have demanded that Jephthah keep his oath to sacrifice his own daughter? Why does God anoint a character like Samson with the divine spirit just so he can execute personal vengeance? Is there, in fact, any one, consistent understanding of God advocated in the book, or is there a multiplicity of understandings reflecting the different stages of composition?

The role of God comes into particular relief where the question of the book's view of kingship is concerned. The period of the judges is presented as a time between the central leadership of Joshua and the rise of kings. The judges are charismatic figures raised up by God. If there is a decline or a vacuum in leadership, therefore, it would appear to be because God has not acted to raise up a new, more effective leader. On the other hand, despite the anticipation at the end of the book that a king will bring order to the present chaos, the early chapters of the next book, 1 Samuel, express divine discontent at the people's cry for a king. Again, this tension has typically been accounted for by scholars as a result of different hands contributing to the development of the constituent parts of the DtrH.

6

1-2 Samuel

The book of Judges ends with the observation that there was no king yet in Israel, leading to the expectation that one would soon be crowned. That expectation is fulfilled in the book of Samuel, which narrates the story of the early monarchy in Israel and its origin. As implied, 1-2 Samuel were originally a single book that was divided in two in the Greek translation of the Hebrew Bible (the Septuagint, abbreviated LXX). The LXX grouped the two books of Samuel together with the books of 1-2 Kings (also originally a single book) to form 1-4 Reigns or Kingdoms. These divisions then became standard in Hebrew Bibles after the sixteenth century c.e.

Contents and Plot

1 Samuel

First Samuel consists of three unequal sections, each one distinguished by its focus on a different main character. The three sections and characters are:

1 Samuel 1–7   Samuel
1 Samuel 8–15   Saul
1 Samuel 16–31   David

This material relates Samuel's birth, training as a priest, and calling as a youth to be a prophet. At the end of this section, Samuel is also depicted as the last of the judges who led Israel. He is, therefore, a transitional figure between the era of the judges and that of the monarchy. Oddly, Samuel is not mentioned in the central part of this section, which is a lengthy story about the capture and return of the ark of the covenant. For that reason, among others, the ark story has often been regarded as a distinct unit or source. The section can be outlined as follows:

> Samuel's birth and dedication to Yahweh's service (1:1–2:11)
> — Hannah's request for a son is answered (1:1-28)
> — The Song of Hannah (2:1-11)
> The rejection of Eli's priestly house (2:12–3:21)
> — The contrast between Eli's sons and Samuel (2:12-26)
> — Eli's house is condemned (2:27-36)
> — Samuel called to prophesy (3:1-21)
> The ark narrative (4:1–7:1)
> — The Philistines capture the ark (4:1-22)
> — The Philistines are ravaged by the ark (5:1-12)
> — The return of the ark (6:1–7:1)
> Samuel judges Israel (7:2-17)

These chapters describe the rise and fall of Saul as Israel's first king, and their contents are organized accordingly in two large segments. Chapters 8–12 portray Saul's anointing as king in stages — first privately, then in a public forum, and finally in response to criticisms, with Saul proving his leadership capabilities and divine charisma on the battlefield. Chapters 13–15 describe Saul's mistakes as king and his rejection. Saul is cast as a tragic figure whose purpose is to pave the way for David. Thus, although Saul still reigns as king at the close of this section, Yahweh has already found his replacement in "a man after his own heart" (13:14). This section may be outlined thus:

> Saul becomes Israel's first king (chs. 8–12)
> — Samuel responds to Israel's cry for a king (8:1-22)

— Saul's private anointing (9:1–10:16)
— Saul is chosen publicly (10:17-27a)
— Saul proves himself in battle (10:27b–11:15)
— Samuel's farewell (12:1-25)
Saul's failings and rejection (chs. 13–15)
— Saul's first disobedience (13:1-22)
— Saul's foolish oath (13:23–14:52)
— Saul's disobedience (15:1-35)

1 SAMUEL 16–31

Comprising over half of the book, this section relates the story of David's rise to the throne. It can be subdivided into segments dealing with his origins, his rise to prominence in Saul's court, and his time on the run from Saul, as in the outline below. In terms of plot, the second segment on David in Saul's court presents an escalation in the overtness of Saul's moves against David that has been obscured by secondary additions in the MT. Thus, Saul tries first to get rid of David by making him a commander in the army in the hope that he will be killed in battle — a plan that backfires because of David's constant success (18:12-16). Next, Saul promotes David's marriage to Michal, again hoping that the Philistines will kill him in his quest for the bride price of one hundred Philistine foreskins (18:20-29). The decisive break between David and Saul occurs when Saul himself tries to kill David with his spear (19:8-10). But this escalation has been obscured in the MT by the insertion of an earlier such attempt (18:10-11) that is absent from the LXX.

David comes to Saul's attention (chs. 16–17)
— David is anointed from among the sheep (16:1-13)
— David is brought to court as Saul's musician (16:14-23)
— David and Goliath (17:1-58)
David in Saul's court (chs. 18–20)
— David's military success (18:1-16)
— David marries Michal (18:17-30)
— Saul moves overtly against David (19:1-24)
— Jonathan warns David (20:1-42)
David the fugitive (chs. 21–31)
— David seeks help from the priests of Nob (21:1-9)

— David feigns madness before the Philistines (21:10-15)
— David gathers an army and provides for his parents (22:1-5)
— Saul's reprisal against Nob (22:6-23)
— David's providential escapes in the wilderness (23:1-29)
— David has a chance to kill Saul (24:1-22)
— David averts a massacre (25:1-44)
— David has another chance to kill Saul (26:1-25)
— David as a Philistine mercenary (27:1–28:2)
— Saul consults a medium (28:3-25)
— The Philistine commanders reject David (29:1-11)
— David avenges the sack of Ziklag (30:1-31)
— Saul and Jonathan die in battle (31:1-13)

2 Samuel

Beginning with another version of Saul's death in battle, 2 Samuel 1 literally takes up where 1 Samuel leaves off. The book recounts David's rise to kingship first over Judah and then over Israel. It describes various activities of David as king relating to the consolidation of his power in Jerusalem and some of his battles with other countries. The affair with Bathsheba is told in the context of one such battle. The bulk of the remainder of the book tells the story of Absalom's revolt. After the report of a second, less successful revolt, the book ends rather abruptly with a collection of materials (narratives, military anecdotes, and poems). David's death is left to be recounted in 1 Kings. Thus, the book of 2 Samuel is comprised of four principal sections:

David's rise to kingship over Israel (1:1–5:5)
David's reign in Jerusalem (5:6–12:31)
Absalom's revolt (chs. 13–20)
Appendix of narratives, military lists, and poems (chs. 21–24)

2 SAMUEL 1:1–5:5

As noted, the first section begins with a reprise of Saul's death, explaining how the news came to David and his response in the form of a lament over Saul and Jonathan. The rest of the section then concerns David's rise to kingship, climaxing in his anointing as king over all Israel. Upon Saul's death, David is made king over Judah. This, plus his overture to the enclave of Saul supporters at Jabesh-gilead provokes Saul's successor Ishbaal into a protracted civil war, which David's forces gradually begin to win. The conclusion to the war comes in the form of two assassinations — that of the enemy commander, Abner, and of Ishbaal himself. Afterward, David becomes king of Israel essentially by default:

> David learns of Saul's death (1:1-27)
> — Interrogation of the Amalekite (1:1-16)
> — David laments Saul and Jonathan (1:17-27)
> Civil war (2:1–5:5)
> — David made king of Judah (2:1-4a)
> — David's letter to Jabesh-Gilead (2:4b-7)
> — Ishbaal made Saul's successor (2:8-11)
> — The battle at Gibeon and the death of Asahel (2:12-32)
> — David's sons born in Hebron (3:1-5)
> — The assassination of Abner (3:6-39)
> — The assassination of Ishbaal (4:1-12)
> — David becomes king of Israel (5:1-5)

2 SAMUEL 5:6–12:31

Section two of 2 Samuel focuses on David's reign — his building of a capital in Jerusalem and his victories over surrounding peoples. The latter is interrupted by the story of his affair with Bathsheba:

> David consolidates the kingdom (5:6-25)
> — Establishing Jerusalem as the capital (5:6-16)
> — Defeating the Philistines (5:17-25)
> David brings the ark to Jerusalem (6:1-23)
> — Transfer of the ark (6:1-19)
> — Encounter with Michal (6:20-23)
> Yahweh's covenant with/promise to David (7:1-29)
> David defeats neighboring countries (8:1-18)
> — David's victories (8:1-14)
> — David's cabinet (8:15-18)
> David's treatment of Mephibosheth (9:1-13)

David's war with the Ammonite-Aramaean coalition (10–12)
— Defeat of the Aramaeans (10:1-19)
— Adultery with Bathsheba and death of Uriah (11:1-27)
— Denunciation and punishment (12:1-25)
— Fall of Rabbat-ammon (12:26-31)

2 SAMUEL 13–20

The third major section in 2 Samuel narrates two revolts — the main one, that of Absalom, followed by a briefer one led by the Benjaminite Sheba. Absalom's revolt appears to have its own immediate cause in the rape of Absalom's sister Tamar by their half brother Amnon. However, as the book now stands, the revolt is punishment for or at least a consequence of David's adultery.

Rape and murder at court (13:1-39)
— Amnon's rape of Tamar (13:1-22)
— Absalom's murder of Amnon (13:23-39)
Absalom's return from exile (14:1-33)
— Intervention of the wise woman of Tekoa (14:1-20)
— Absalom's return (14:21-33)
Absalom seizes the throne (15:1–16:23)
Absalom's defeat and death (17:1–18:18)
David's reaction and return to Jerusalem (18:19–19:43)
Sheba's revolt (20:1-26)
— Amasa's assassination (20:1-13)
— Sheba's demise (20:14-22)
— David's cabinet (20:23-26)

2 SAMUEL 21–24

The concluding section of 2 Samuel is a kind of appendix — a collection of narratives, anecdotes, lists, and poems. The arrangement of these materials, however, is not haphazard but quite deliberate and balanced, as the outline below indicates.

Narrative: The execution of Saul's heirs (21:1-14)
Military anecdotes: Heroes of the Philistine wars (21:15-22)

77

Poem: David's song of deliverance (22:1-51)
Poem: David's last words (23:1-7)
Military anecdotes: David's military honor roll (23:8-39)
Narrative: David's census (24:1-25)

Composition and Literary History

The book of Samuel is obviously named after the prophet Samuel, who is traditionally viewed as its author. The preceding overview of the book's contents shows how inappropriate the name and attribution are, since Samuel is the focal character only in the first eight chapters of 1 Samuel. What is more, he dies before 1 Samuel ends (25:1) and is not mentioned at all in 2 Samuel. The Babylonian Talmud (sixth century C.E.) dealt with this inappropriateness by assigning Samuel the authorship of those parts of the book that treat events before his death and consigning the rest to the prophets Nathan and Gad based on the mention of their "records" in 1 Chr 29:29.

As we saw in Chapter Two above, scholarship since the 1940s has tended to view Samuel, along with Deuteronomy and the other Former Prophets (Joshua, Judges, and Kings) as part of the anonymous Deuteronomistic History (DtrH), a single, extended history of Israel from Moses to the exile. Thus, Samuel continues the story from Judges, presenting Samuel as a judge. By the same token, the story in Samuel is continued in Kings, which begins with David's pending death and the question of who is to succeed him. It is worth observing in this regard that David, by virtue of both the placement of the material about him in Samuel and of its length, is the central and principal character of the DtrH. There are also some distinctly Dtr texts in Samuel. For instance, 1 Samuel 8 and 12 have long been recognized as Dtr's handiwork. The references to bringing Israel up out of Egypt (8:8) and the people crying out (8:18) as well as the review of Israel's history and the command to heed Yahweh's voice (12:14-15) are typical of Dtr's style and language. Of even greater significance is the account of the covenant promising David an enduring dynasty in 2 Samuel 7. Not only is this text as it now stands thoroughly Dtr in nature, but it is also a crucial passage for Dtr's theology, as we will see in the next chapter on Kings.

In spite of these strong indications of Dtr's presence in Samuel, scholars have long observed that there are substantial portions of the book that lack evidence of Dtr input, thus creating something of a paradox. Aside from denying the existence of the DtrH, which is an option taken by some, scholars have dealt with this paradox in one of three ways, used either individually or in combination with each other. The first and most common approach to this matter is the postulation of older sources used by Dtr. The classic form of this approach is that of Leonhard Rost, who theorized three such sources — a "Succession Narrative" behind 2 Samuel 9–20 and 1 Kings 1–2, which dealt with the question of who would succeed David; an "Ark Narrative" behind 1 Sam 4:1–7:1 + 2 Samuel 6; and a "History of David's Rise" underlying 1 Samuel 16–2 Samuel 5.[1] This theory, once widely accepted, has come under attack in recent decades because of the difficulty inherent in defining the precise boundaries of these sources and dubiousness about the early date Rost ascribed to them. In the case of the "Succession Narrative," it has also been observed that at the least this is a misnomer, since only the final part of it (1 Kings 1–2) is really focused on the issue of David's succession.

The second approach is the contention that there is more evidence of Dtr activity in the relevant section(s) of Samuel than customarily admitted. In the case of the "Succession Narrative," this approach is associated with the Finnish scholar Timo Veijola, who assumed the existence of the older narrative source but sought to show that the Dtr editors had been more involved in editing the material for their own purposes than scholars had generally allowed.[2] Regarding the "History of David's Rise," John Van Seters has argued that there is no need to posit an underlying narrative source at all and that this material is best seen simply as Dtr's creation.[3]

The third way in which scholars have tried to resolve the paradox of Samuel is also identified with Van Seters, this time in reference to the "Suc-

---

1. Leonhard Rost, *Die Überlieferung von der Thronnachfolge Davids*. BWANT 3/6 (Stuttgart: Kohlhammer, 1926) = *The Succession to the Throne of David*. Historic Texts and Interpreters in Biblical Scholarship (Sheffield: Almond, 1982).

2. Timo Veijola, *Die ewige Dynastie: David und die Entstehung seiner Dynastie nach der deuteronomistischen Darstellung*. AASF B 193 (Helsinki: Suomalainen Tiedeakatemia, 1975). As an adherent of the "Smend" or "Göttingen" approach to the DtrH (see Chapter Two above), Veijola held the view that there were different layers of Dtr editing in Samuel, though he mostly assigned material to the basic Historian identified with Noth's Dtr.

3. John Van Seters, *In Search of History: Historiography in the Ancient World and the Origins of Biblical History* (New Haven: Yale University Press, 1983) 264-71. Van Seters does not deny that Dtr may have had source material, only that there was no extended, running narrative underlying essentially 1 Samuel 16–2 Samuel 5.

cession Narrative."[4] Van Seters recognizes the inadequacy of this moniker and prefers the designation "Court History" for the material identified by Rost. Then, he proposes that this material is not a pre-Dtr source but an addition to Dtr's History, which ended its account of David with 2 Samuel 7.[5] He can thus account for Dtr language either as material coming from Dtr's hand or as the imitation of Dtr style. Van Seters also finds examples of tensions between Dtr ideology and that of the "Court History." Such tensions, he reasons, must be post-Dtr additions, since Dtr would not have allowed them to stand uncorrected from one of his sources. It is this post-Dtr author, Van Seters thinks, who not only added the "Court History" but who also added materials to 1 Samuel thereby creating a new work — the "David Saga," presently in 1-2 Samuel.

The different theories just surveyed indicate the complicated nature of the question of Samuel's composition. While the matters of the existence of these theoretical narrative sources and Dtr's relationship to them must remain open, it can be demonstrated both that Dtr used sources and that there were post-Dtr additions and changes in Samuel. In other words, there is clear confirmation that the book's compositional history was complicated. The series of stories about Saul becoming king in 1 Samuel 9–11 well illustrate Dtr's use of sources. There are three distinct stories here: 9:1–10:16, in which Saul goes in search of lost donkeys and is anointed king; 10:17-27a, in which Saul is publicly designated king in an assembly at Mizpah; and 10:27b–11:15, in which Saul leads Israel to victory over the Ammonites and is proclaimed king at Gilgal.

The presence of an older story or tradition that has been at least updated seems indisputable considering 1 Sam 9:9, which reads: "Formerly in Israel, anyone who went to inquire of God would say, 'Come, let us go to the seer'; for the one who is now called a prophet was formerly called a seer" (NRSV). Note that the NRSV places this verse in parentheses — appropriately so, for it obviously interrupts the narration of the story. Its

4. In addition to the section of *In Search of History* just cited, see Van Seters, "The Court History and DtrH," in *Die sogenannte Thronfolgegeschichte Davids: Neue Einsichten und Anfragen*, ed. Albert de Pury and Thomas Römer. OBO 176 (Freiburg: Universitäts-verlag, 2000) 70-93. Van Seters's fullest explanation of his position is in his most recent book, *The Biblical Saga of King David* (Winona Lake: Eisenbrauns, 2009).

5. In Van Seters's view, the author of the "Court History" or "David Saga" shifted the material now in 2 Samuel 8 from its place in the DtrH before 2 Samuel 7. Van Seters's view is articulated fully in *The Biblical Saga*.

purpose is to define the term "seer," which was evidently used in the older story but which the author thought might be unfamiliar to his audience.

There are other tensions and points of unevenness within the present narrative that indicate reworking. Most notable among them is the fact that Samuel is not initially referred to by name but by profession as "a man of God" (9:6). Neither Saul nor his servant seems to know who Samuel is, despite the fact that the first eight chapters of the book establish his identity as Israel's national leader at the time. This suggests that the story may originally have been about a nameless prophet who was not specifically identified with Samuel; that identification arose later. There is also a curious tension between v. 19 and v. 20. Samuel first tells Saul that he (Samuel) will give Saul all the information he seeks the next morning, after Saul has spent the night at Samuel's house. What Saul and his servant seek at this point is the whereabouts of their lost donkeys. So it is odd that in the very next breath, or at least the next verse, Samuel tells Saul that the donkeys have been found and that he need not worry about them any longer.

These tensions indicate that the original version of this story was a tale about Saul searching for some lost donkeys and encountering a nameless man of God who helps him by finding out through supernatural means that the donkeys have been found. In the original tale, the man of God apparently needed to inquire of God and receive a dream or other form of revelation overnight in order to inform Saul of the whereabouts of his donkeys. This tale was transformed into a story of Saul's anointing and the man of God identified as the prophet Samuel. The entire focus of the story was similarly shifted from the matter of the lost donkeys to Saul's anointing as king. Thus, the problem of the lost donkeys was dispensed with in v. 20 so that Saul's anointing becomes the focus of the scene between Samuel and Saul the next morning (9:27–10:1).

Saul's anointing in this story is a private affair between him and Samuel alone; even the servant does not know about it because he is sent on ahead. By way of reinforcing this point, at the conclusion of the story is an anecdote about an interview Saul has with his uncle upon his return home (10:14-16). The writer takes pains to point out that Saul told his uncle about the donkeys but not a word about his anointing. The uncle is an unusual choice as Saul's conversation partner here, since it was Saul's father who sent him on the errand to find the donkeys and the uncle has no other involvement in the story. These features suggest that the interview is an addition by the author of the story who used the old tale as a source.

The function of the addition is to reinforce the private nature of Saul's anointing in order to prepare the reader for the next story, in which Saul is publicly made king.

In the second story about how Saul became king, he is chosen through a lot-casting ceremony at a national assembly (10:17-27a). Some scholars think there is an older tale beneath this second story as well — a tale in which Saul was chosen for his height (10:23). This is more speculative, however. The fact that Saul hides suggests that he thinks he will be chosen before the lot is cast, which in turn suggests that this story presupposes the previous one. If so, 10:17-27a may be a Dtr composition. Another indication of this is the fact that the assembly takes place at Mizpah. This detail seems to reflect not an early circumstance as one might expect in an older source, but a situation contemporary with Dtr, since Mizpah became an administrative center only after the destruction of Jerusalem and the beginning of the exile (2 Kgs 25:23). In any case, at the end of the story, there is a notice about certain disgruntled individuals who complain about Saul and disdain his ability to rescue them from their enemies (1 Sam 10:27a). This notice functions in a way similar to that about the interview between Saul and his uncle. It prepares the reader for the next story in the series, which will answer the objection of those who were disgruntled by demonstrating that Saul was an effective military leader who could save Israel from its enemies.

The third story has its original beginning in the verse represented as 1 Sam 10:27b in the NRSV. This verse is not found in most English Bibles; the NRSV is an exception. That is because the verse was accidentally lost from the MT of Samuel. It was restored in the NRSV on the basis of the Dead Sea Scroll manuscript 4QSam^a, where it is preserved in fragmentary form. The information it gives, however, is crucial for understanding the background to this story. That background is as follows. The Ammonite king, Nahash, was oppressing Israelites from the tribes of Gad and Reuben who lived east of the Jordan in territory Nahash claimed for Ammon. He displayed his dominion over them by gouging out their right eyes. His attack on Jabesh-gilead, which lay outside of the disputed territory, came about because some Gadites and Reubenites fled there.

For our present purposes, what is most important is that the story obviously does not presuppose that Saul is king. When Nahash gives the Jabesh-gileadites the opportunity to seek help, they do not send directly to Saul, as one would expect if he had been king. Rather, Saul is working in the field as a commoner. He only learns of Jabesh's predicament because messengers from there happen to pass through Gibeah, Saul's home town, and he happens to hear people reacting to the news the messengers bring (11:3-6). When he hears the messengers' story, he is moved by the spirit of God to lead Israel into battle.

Thus, in the original version of the story, Saul's victory in battle was what led to his being made king. This is, in effect, what 11:15 says — all the people went to Gilgal and made Saul king there. However, the story has been edited with the addition of vv. 12-14 in order to connect it to the foregoing stories of Saul's becoming king. Verse 14 alters the language, stating that Saul's kingship was *renewed* in Gilgal. Verses 12-13 refer back to 10:27a and the individuals who questioned Saul's capabilities, thereby nicely linking the present story in with the previous one, such that here in 10:27b–11:15 Saul answers the doubts raised about him at the end of 10:17-27a.

Of the three distinct stories in 1 Samuel 9–11, then, the first and third are definitely based on older, independent tales that have been revised through editing. All three have then been put together, again through editing, to produce an account of Saul's becoming king in three stages — privately, publicly, and by acclamation following a charismatic military victory. The editor/reviser was Dtr, as indicated by the speeches in chs. 8 and 12 that enclose this unit and that are long-recognized Dtr compositions.

The post-Dtr changes can also be demonstrated both text-critically and redaction-critically. The text-critical situation of 1 Samuel 17, in which the LXX indicates that the MT is conflate, also pertains in the next chapter. Specifically, 18:1-5, 10-11, 17-19, 29b-30 are absent from the LXX, and source-critical criteria indicate that they are additions to the MT. We have already seen that 18:1-5 interrupts the continuity between the Goliath story and the army's return following that battle in 18:6. We have also seen that Saul's attempt to spear David in 18:10-11 anticipates a later anecdote (19:8-10) and ruins the gradual increase in the overtness of Saul's attempts on David's life in the original plot. Similarly, Saul's withdrawal of the offer of his daughter Merab (18:17-19) is a doublet of the Michal story which follows it, and the note about David's success in the army (18:29b-30) rehearses much of 18:12-16.

There are other, fairly obvious cases of literary revision in Samuel, but since the LXX is not a factor, it is not certain that these are post-Dtr changes. One of the best examples is the story of the famine during David's reign and his subsequent execution of almost all of Saul's male heirs

(2 Sam 21:1-14). This story apparently once stood immediately before 2 Samuel 9:1, where David asks whether anyone is left of Saul's house. The question makes the most sense after the execution of most of the male members of Saul's house. In addition, the duplicate cabinet list in 8:15-18 and 20:23-26 seems to be a remnant of the original placement. In other words, someone moved the story in 21:1-14 from its original location, placing it in its present spot in the miscellaneous collection of the final four chapters of 2 Samuel.

In sum, it is clear that the book of Samuel has had a long and complex literary history, both before Dtr's composition and after, even if scholars have not yet succeeded in completely unraveling that history in all its stages.

As indicated by the treatment of 1 Samuel 17 in Chapter Three, the textual history of Samuel is an important part of the book's development. The Dead Sea Scrolls, especially the 4QSam[a] fragments, have been revolutionary in enhancing scholars' understanding of this textual history. They generally show closer agreement with the LXX and Chronicles parallels than with the MT of Samuel. They thus demonstrated the great value of the LXX as a textual witness. In Samuel, in fact, the LXX appears to preserve a better text than the MT, which has a tendency toward haplography, i.e., accidental omissions.

Reading Strategies and Interpretation

The book of Samuel essentially tells a single story, so it is probably best read as such, i.e., from start to finish. This reading may be enriched in the same ways that apply to the reading of any story and that thus cultivate an appreciation of the book as literature. For instance, it is useful to keep in mind that the story is told by an "omniscient narrator," who relates such details as private conversations and characters' personal thoughts. Then, as with any great literature, Samuel is full of wordplays, intricate plots with subtle twists, and portraits of complex characters. Minute, seemingly meaningless details can sometimes shed an entirely new light on events or characters.

The characters and the way they are portrayed are a major element in Samuel's story. The book presents a bewildering array of new names and characters, so that it is helpful to keep tabs on their identities and relationships. Characterization takes place on different levels. One level is that of physical descriptions. In contrast to modern stories, physical descriptions of characters are rare in the Bible. They are virtually nonexistent for Adam and Eve, Moses, Jesus, Paul, and most others. Descriptions are more frequent in Samuel than elsewhere in the Bible — though still not as common as in modern novels. Samuel has at least partial descriptions of Saul, David, Absalom, and Abigail, for instance, but still none of Jonathan, Michal, Joab, Solomon, or most others. When descriptions are given, they should be noted, as they will likely play some role in the plot of the story.

A more significant dimension of characterization in the Bible relates to a character's inner qualities and motives. This is especially the case in Samuel, where such qualities and motives are typically revealed by characters' actions or speeches, and often there is ambiguity, especially where David is concerned. A key question to ask is which character(s) benefit from events that are reported and whether those characters may have been responsible for bringing about the events in question. Again, this is an especially useful technique where David is concerned.

There is widespread recognition that the story of David's rise in 1 Samuel 16–2 Samuel 5 is strongly pro-David. As observed, David is, in a real sense, the central hero of the DtrH. Saul serves as a foil to David; he can do nothing right, while David can do no wrong. It is not entirely clear, for instance, exactly what Saul does wrong in either 1 Samuel 13 or 15. In the former story, he is accused of disobedience. But he waits seven days for Samuel, according to Samuel's instructions, and he only offers the sacrifice himself when Samuel is late. In ch. 15, he is told to annihilate the Amalekites, and he does so except for the king and the best of the animals. But he tells Samuel that he intends to sacrifice the animals, which would presumably fulfill the order to slaughter them all, and there is some indication that he is saving the Amalekite king for ritual execution, which he ultimately receives at Samuel's hands. The point of both stories seems to be simply to get rid of Saul, even if on something of a pretense, in favor of David.

Thus, in ch. 16 the spirit of God abandons Saul and comes upon David, and from then on the point is constantly made that Yahweh is with David. This is stated in 16:18 and illustrated in the Goliath story. During David's time at court, Saul is depicted as irrational and insanely jealous. Everyone else — including Saul's own children — loves David. When David flees and is on the run from Saul in chs. 21–31, the theme of Yahweh's presence with David and opposition to Saul continues. The nadir of Saul's relationship with God comes early on, in ch. 22, when he slaughters Yahweh's priests at Nob, thus in effect waging "holy war" against God. David, by contrast, consistently consults Yahweh and receives guidance about what moves to make. Even in a story like the one in 23:24-28, which does not explicitly mention God, the hint of divine help is clear, as David is trapped by Saul and escapes only at the last moment. Twice, in chs. 24 and 26, Yahweh even delivers Saul over to David, but David, for reasons of piety and loyalty, refuses to extend his hand against Yahweh's anointed.

A common reading strategy for this material is to regard it as apologetic in nature and tone. An apology in this sense is a literary defense or legitimation. That is, part of the work's purpose, at least at some level in its development, was to defend David in the face of accusations about his character, actions, and status. Above all, the story seems concerned to confront the charge that David usurped the throne from Saul. This charge is countered, in part, by the observation that David, though not Saul's direct heir, had some claim to succession by virtue of being his son-in-law. More importantly, however, the story in 1 Samuel files the claim that David was chosen by God to replace Saul as king.

Not only was David chosen by God and not a usurper, but the entire section of 1 Samuel 24–31 seems designed to respond to the allegation that David was involved in Saul's death. Thus, in chs. 24 and 26, he twice declines to kill Saul when he has the chance, implying that he would not have done so ultimately. In between (ch. 25) is a story in which he is prevented from annihilating the Saul-like figure Nabal. The stories about David among the Philistines (chs. 27; 29) explain that David did not go to war with the Philistines against Saul and demonstrate his continuing loyalty to Saul and his deception of the Philistines, so that if he had participated in the battle, it would have been on Saul's side. Saul's interview with the medium in Endor (ch. 28) shows that Saul's fate was sealed before the battle began. Chapter 30 places David far away, dealing with his own problems when Saul was wounded in battle and then took his own life (ch. 31).

A significant concern for the apologist was the series of corpses that evidently littered David's path toward kingship. The list begins with Nabal and then Saul and Jonathan, but there are many others. They are followed in 2 Samuel by Abner (ch. 3) and Ishbaal (ch. 4). The apologetic nature of the story of Abner's assassination seems especially patent in the author's constant reminder to the reader that Joab acted alone for personal reasons, without the consent or knowledge of David. Thus, the reader is assured that David dismissed Abner and he had left David's presence in peace (3:21, 22, 23, 24), that Joab acted alone without David's consent or knowledge when he summoned Abner to return (3:26), and that Joab murdered Abner for reasons of personal vengeance and not on David's orders (3:27). Furthermore, David condemned Joab's act in no uncertain terms, cursed him for it (3:28, 29), and mourned profusely for Abner (3:31-35) to the point that all the people were convinced that he had nothing to do with the murder (3:36, 37).

There is a pattern of sorts that emerges in these stories. A prominent man who stands in the way of David's acquisition or maintenance of power dies violently. The narrative asserts that David had nothing to do with the death, and as part of that assertion describes him as mourning profusely when he hears the news. Such is the case certainly with the deaths of Saul and Jonathan and the murder of Abner. The story about Ishbaal's assassination resembles the second account of Saul's death in 2 Samuel 1 in that as the one explains how David ended up with the crown without having killed Saul, the other has David end up with Ishbaal's head without being involved in his assassination.

There is less unanimity among scholars about how to read 2 Samuel, especially the so-called Succession Narrative in 2 Samuel 9–20. In my view and that of many others, the apologetic tendency of 1 Samuel continues, defending David in the face of suspicions that he killed off most of Saul's heirs, his own sons, Amnon and Absalom, and his nephew Amasa, all of whom threaten David's maintenance of power in some way. As with Nabal, Saul and Jonathan, Abner, and Ishbaal, they all perish through violent means, according to the narrative, though never by David's own hand or order. As in the case of Abner, Joab bears the blame for the murders of Absalom (2 Sam 18:1-15) and Amasa (20:4-10), against David's orders. While Joab and his fellow "sons of Zeruiah" are harsh and violent men, David is portrayed as too tender for such deeds (16:10; 19:22; cf. 3:39), and he is deeply grieved by Absalom's death as he was by Abner's (3:31-37; 18:22–19:8). In the case of Absalom's death, as in those of Saul and Jonathan and Abner, David's mourning is described in great detail.

A reading of the story of David's execution of Saul's sons and grandsons in 21:1-14 as apology seems particularly appropriate. According to the story, David is compelled to order their executions because of a famine resulting from a misdeed by Saul himself that must be requited by blood vengeance. The misdeed is a violation of the treaty with the Gibeonites forged in Joshua 9. However, there is no account of any attempt by Saul to exterminate the Gibeonites anywhere in the DtrH. In addition, the fact that it was common practice for a usurper to annihilate the males in the line of his predecessor (see the next chapter on Kings) strongly suggests that David's execution of Saul's heirs was politically motivated. Only Mephibosheth, who is disabled and therefore less of a threat, is spared, and David keeps a watchful eye on him by bringing him to the king's house (2 Samuel 9). The fact that 21:1-14 probably immediately preceded 9:1 at one stage (cf. pp. 83-84 above) further supports the political interpretation, as annihilating the preceding dynasty was a step typically undertaken early on in a usurper's reign.

The one story in 2 Samuel that cannot be read apologetically is that of David's adultery with Bathsheba (chs. 11–12). The contrast with the rest of the book is instructive. There is no attempt to legitimate or explain away David's actions. He alone bears the blame. It seems likely that 2 Samuel 11–12 are a later addition. A further indication of this possibility is the fact that, while they contain allusions to events in subsequent chapters (12:11-12), the later stories never refer back to the Bathsheba event. Moreover, the presence of the Bathsheba material completely alters the way in which the subsequent material is read. Absalom's revolt, which has its own cause apart from the Bathsheba story in Amnon's rape of Tamar (ch. 13), now becomes an extension of the punishment leveled against David because of sin. Thus, the Bathsheba story is not part of the apology for David but part of the literary development of Samuel at a later stage.

As hinted, not all scholars read 2 Samuel through an apologetic lens. Some see the David story as falling into two major sections — blessing and curse — the dividing point being the Bathsheba story. Some believe that David is portrayed as a model, albeit flawed figure throughout. This perspective reads 2 Samuel 11–20 more or less at face value with David as a good man and ruler whose weaknesses emerge in his inability to control his children. Part of the reason for this problem is the bad example he provides of being unable to control his appetites where Bathsheba is concerned. Even here, though, it is argued that David exemplifies repentance, which is immediately accepted because of his faithfulness otherwise (12:13). Yet another perspective sees the Court History as a rejoinder to the DtrH in its positive portrayal of David, offering instead a scathing condemnation of the Davidic line and even of monarchy in general.[6] Perhaps

6. See the references to the works of Van Seters in notes 3 and 4.

it is fair to say that 2 Samuel in its current form depicts David as a complex, highly ambiguous character who defies simple explanation.

History

The debate over the historicity of the David story has often been heated. It is fueled by the fact that there are a number of factors to consider, making it quite a complex matter. To begin, no reference to the person of David outside of the Bible and materials dependent on it has ever been found, suggesting to some scholars that David was not a historical figure. It was not until 1993 that David's name was first discovered in an ancient source outside of the Bible — a ninth-century Aramaic inscription found at Tel Dan in northern Israel. Even then, the name occurred as part of an expression, "the house of David," referring to Judah and its ruling house. The discovery was an important one, for it lends a great deal of weight to the likelihood of David's historical existence. But it certainly does not mean that all of Samuel is historical, and the inscription tells us nothing about the details of David's life.

The interpretation of the archaeological evidence regarding David's reign is also disputed. In fact, there is no archaeological evidence to speak of for David. The dispute is over finds, largely architectural, that have been attributed to Solomon. Some have argued recently that the relevant sites were misdated and that they should be attributed to the ninth-century Omride dynasty rather than to Solomon.[7] While Jerusalem's existence in the tenth century is beyond dispute, many think it was little more than the village home of a clan or chiefdom.

The date and nature of the literature in Samuel are integral elements in this debate. As part of the DtrH, Samuel was written, apart from later additions, in the sixth century B.C.E., hundreds of years after David. Earlier scholars, like Rost, believed the sources they postulated, especially the "Succession Narrative," to have been written virtually at the same time as the events they related. However, as we have seen, the dimensions, early

---

7. See esp. the following two recent books by Israel Finkelstein and Neil Asher Silberman: *The Bible Unearthed: Archaeology's New Vision of Ancient Israel and the Origin of Its Sacred Texts* (New York: Free Press, 2001); and *David and Solomon: In Search of the Bible's Sacred Kings and the Roots of the Western Tradition* (New York: Free Press, 2006).

date, and bare existence of these hypothetical sources have been called into question. The apologetic nature of the David story suggests a means of getting at history. For instance, a narrative that "protests too much" might lead the historical critic to conclude that the historical reality was the reverse of the case the author wishes to make. We have already seen how the claim that David's execution of Saul's heirs was not politically motivated hints at just the opposite. Similarly, the fact that 1 Samuel 24–31 seems focused on showing that David would not and could not have been involved in any attempt on Saul's life might convince the modern critic that there was something to this accusation. Again, the benefit David derived from Abner's death and the narrative's repeated assertion that David dismissed Abner in peace and knew nothing about Joab's plan to murder him suggests David's involvement. At the same time, the strong pro-David orientation of the Samuel story raises questions about the extent to which history may have been forfeited to or shaped by authorial interests. Additionally, the literary creativity the book exhibits — its puns and word plays, complex characters, and intricate plots, for example — also raises questions about the extent to which historicity has been sacrificed to artistry.

It is worth noting in closing that even if all of Samuel were historical, it would still report only a very small amount of David's actual life and reign. To take 2 Samuel as an example, there are forty years attributed to David's reign. That figure is likely a round number for a generation. In any case, the book relates only a handful of events during that span of time, concentrating most of its attention on Absalom's revolt. With such a paucity of information from any and all sources, any historical reconstruction is by necessity a mere silhouette of reality at best.

7

1-2 Kings

Like 1-2 Samuel, 1-2 Kings are two parts of a single book. This is indicated by the fact that the present division between the two books comes in the middle of the reign of King Ahaziah of Israel. Moreover, as observed in Chapter Two above, Kings was likely written not as a distinct work but as part of the much larger Deuteronomistic History (DtrH), which comprises Deuteronomy plus the Former Prophets (Joshua, Judges, 1-2 Samuel, and 1-2 Kings). Hence, 1 Kings continues with the same events and characters as 1-2 Samuel. The LXX regards 1-2 Samuel and 1-2 Kings as four parts of the same work entitled Kingdoms *(Basileiōn)* 1-4, and some Greek manuscripts place the division between Samuel and Kings after 1 Kgs 2:11, suggesting the arbitrary nature of the separation of the books.

Contents, Structure, and Purpose

As its title indicates, the book of Kings recounts the history of the Israelite and Judahite monarchies. Its content is comprised of three large sections:

1 Kings 1–11	Reign of Solomon
1 Kings 12–2 Kings 17	History of the divided kingdoms
2 Kings 18–25	Judah alone after the fall of Israel

Each of these sections, in turn, has its own structure and/or organizational scheme, so that they are best treated separately.

Reign of Solomon

The account of Solomon's reign exhibits a clear structure that may be diagramed in the following way:

A. Transfer and consolidation of the kingdom (1 Kings 1–2)
   B. Solomon's wisdom (1 Kings 3–4)
      C. Building and dedication of the temple (1 Kings 5–8)
   B'. Solomon's wealth (1 Kings 9–10)
A'. Solomon's apostasy (1 Kings 11)

This type of arrangement is known as a chiasm or chiastic structure. From the Greek letter *chi* (χ), the term refers to a literary arrangement in which the components correspond to one another from the outside in, such that the central component is the crux or focus of the author's or editor's product. In the case of the Solomon material, the components labeled A and A' correspond because the first two chapters describe Solomon's acquisition of the kingdom through succession to David, and ch. 11 describes the sin that led God to announce the loss of the kingdom after Solomon's death. The components B and B' correspond in their illustration of Solomon's attributes of wisdom and wealth and their impact on his kingdom. The focal point of the account of Solomon, though, is clearly his building and dedication of the temple in component C. This is the central component and the largest of the narratives about Solomon, and it exhibits the author's concern for religious and cultic matters.

History of the Divided Kingdoms

The second major section of Kings relates the events surrounding the division of Israel and Judah (1 Kings 12) and then narrates their history as separate but related kingdoms. The division is portrayed as a secession on Israel's part led by Jeroboam (12:1-24), who, as Israel's first king, led his people into apostasy by founding two shrines to rival Jerusalem (12:25-33). This "sin of Jeroboam" is seen as having an enduring, detrimental impact on the northern kingdom throughout its history.

The simultaneous histories of Israel and Judah following their division may be outlined as follows:

Israel	Judah
The house of Jeroboam Jeroboam (13:1–14:20)	
	Rehoboam (14:21-31)
	Abijam (15:1-8)
	Asa (15:9-24)
Nadab (15:25-32)	
The house of Baasha Baasha (15:33–16:7)	
Elah (16:8-14)	
Zimri (16:15-20)	
The house of Omri Omri (16:21-28)	
Ahab's accession (16:29-34) Stories about Elijah (chs. 17–19) Prophetic story (ch. 20) Naboth's vineyard (ch. 21) Prophetic story (22:1-38) Ahab's closing formulas (22:39-40)	
	Jehoshaphat (22:41-50)
Ahaziah (22:51–2 Kgs 1:18)	
Elisha inherits Elijah's spirit (2 Kings 2)	
Joram's accession (3:1-3) Stories about Elisha (3:4–8:15)	
	Jehoram (8:16-24)
	Ahaziah's accession (8:25-29)
The house of Jehu Jehu's revolt and reign (chs. 9–10)	Jehu's revolt (chs. 9–10)
	Athaliah's interregnum (ch. 11)

Joash (ch. 12)

Jehoahaz (13:1-9)

Jehoash (13:10-13)

Elisha's death (13:14-25)

Amaziah (14:1-22)

Jeroboam (14:23-29)

Azariah/Uzziah (15:1-7)

Zechariah (15:8-12)

Shallum (15:13-16)

The house of Menahem
    Menahem (15:17-22)

    Pekahiah (15:23-26)

Pekah (15:27-31)

Jotham (15:32-38)

Ahaz (ch. 16)

Hoshea and the fall of Israel (ch. 17)

The outline shows that the narrative in Kings essentially alternates between the two kingdoms. Each king's reign is dated according to the regnal years of a counterpart in the other kingdom, such that the histories of the two kingdoms are intertwined until the fall of Israel (2 Kings 17).

The **regnal formulas** for each king form the framework for the narratives about him. That is, there is an opening and a closing formula for each king, and whatever narrative, if any, that the book includes for that king's reign comes between the two formulas. The usual opening formula for Israelite kings contains three elements: (1) an accession statement giving the name of the king and his patronymic (father's name) and dating the beginning of his reign according to his counterpart in Judah; (2) the length of his reign; and (3) an evaluation in religious terms. For example, the opening formula for Jehoahaz (2 Kgs 13:1-2), identifying its constituent elements, reads:

Accession: "In the twenty-third year of King Joash son of Ahaziah of Judah, Jehoahaz son of Jehu began to reign over Israel in Samaria;"

Length: "he reigned seventeen years."

Evaluation: "He did what was evil in the sight of Yahweh, and followed the sins of Jeroboam son of Nebat, which he caused Israel to sin; he did not depart from them."

Notably, every king of Israel is given a negative evaluation, and most are accused of perpetuating the "sin(s) of Jeroboam" or walking in the "way of Jeroboam."

The opening formulas for the kings of Judah typically mention the king's age at accession and the name of the Queen Mother in addition to the same three elements occurring in the formulas for the Israelite kings. Several of the evaluations for the kings of Judah also make a comparison with David, and some focus on the king's treatment of the "high places" (Hebrew *bāmôt*) or shrines outside of Jerusalem. Eight kings of Judah are evaluated as righteous in Yahweh's eyes. They are, in order: Asa, Jehoshaphat, Joash, Amaziah, Azariah, Jotham, Hezekiah, and Josiah. There are no formulas for Athaliah, signaling the author's view that her reign was illegitimate.

The closing formulas for the kings of both countries typically begin with a rhetorical question referring the reader to the "book of the annals" of the kings of Israel or Judah. These formulas often include the idiom "slept with his fathers" as a reference to the king's death, and they sometimes mention the place of the king's burial and the name of his son who succeeded him. They occasionally supply other details about the expired king's reign or manner of death.

In addition to the regnal formulas, another organizational scheme operating in this section of Kings is that of **prophecy and fulfillment**. In this scheme, a series of prophecies against the northern dynasties or royal houses of Jeroboam, Baasha, and Omri/Ahab (1 Kgs 14:7-18; 16:1-4; 21:20-24) occur in the book, followed by notices of their fulfillments (1 Kgs 15:27-30; 16:11-13; 2 Kgs 9:1–10:17). The prophecies threaten the extinction of the ruling house through the assassination and nonburial of its male members. They have several expressions in common with each other and with their fulfillment notices. Among these, they typically speak of "cutting off" every male, "bond or free," belonging to the dynasty founder, and they use an idiom for male that literally means "one who urinates on the wall." The threat of nonburial is expressed as consumption by animals — those who die in cities being eaten by dogs and those who die in open country by birds. The language and expressions that these prophecies and fulfillments have in common show that they were composed by the same author, the Deuteronomistic Historian (Dtr). They offer an etiological explanation for the series of military coups in Israel's history, each one establishing a new dynasty.[1] Why Dtr chose not to apply the scheme to the final father-son succession of Menahem and Pekahiah is not clear, but it may have something to do with the extensive narrative of Jehu's overthrow of the Omri dynasty and the assassination of Jezebel (2 Kings 9–10), part of which Dtr inherited and used as the climax of this scheme.

Judah Alone

The third section of Kings continues with the kingdom of Judah after the fall of Israel. It is structured according to the reigns of the kings as follows:

Hezekiah (2 Kings 18–20)
Manasseh (21:1-18)
Amon (21:19-26)
Josiah (22:1–23:30)
Jehoahaz (23:31-35)
Jehoiakim (23:36–24:7)
Jehoiachin (24:8-17)
Zedekiah (24:18–25:7)

The book ends with the destruction of Jerusalem and the exile of Judah to Babylon (25:8-21), followed by notices regarding the appointment of Gedaliah as governor (25:22-26) and the release of Jehoiachin from prison and elevation to the table of the king of Babylon (25:27-30). The relative importance that Dtr attaches to these kings may be indicated by the quantity of material devoted to each. The longest narratives by far are those

1. For further discussion, see Steven L. McKenzie, *The Trouble with Kings: The Composition of the Book of Kings in the Deuteronomistic History.* VTSup 42 (Leiden: Brill, 1991) 61-80.

about Hezekiah and Josiah, who are both important reforming kings. The next longest is that of Manasseh, but for the opposite reason. That is, Manasseh is regarded in Kings as the worst king of Judah, whose wickedness was so great that he sealed the fate of the nation, and even Josiah could not prevent its destruction.

The structure of the book of Kings, particularly the prophecy-fulfillment scheme, is a crucial consideration for discerning the book's purpose, which, as shown in Chapter Two above, is in turn crucial for discerning the purpose, date, and authorship of the entire DtrH. The prophecy-fulfillment scheme highlights the major contrast between Israel's history and Judah's: Judah was ruled by a single dynasty (David's) throughout its history, while Israel went through a series of royal houses. The reason for this difference, according to Kings, was the Israelite kings' perpetuation of the "sin of Jeroboam." This sin was Jeroboam's erection of two royal shrines in the northern kingdom, as explained in 1 Kgs 12:25-33. In other words, the northern kings continued the practice of worshipping at the national shrines that were established by Jeroboam, and this sin was the cause for the downfall of each successive dynasty in Israel and ultimately for the nation's destruction (2 Kgs 17:21-23).

Dtr also used prophecy and fulfillment to account for the endurance of David's dynasty in Judah. In this case, the prophecy was the oracle by the prophet Nathan in 2 Samuel 7 promising David an "eternal house" for his faithfulness. The Hebrew word "forever" *(lĕ-* or *ʿad-ʿôlām)*, which is used here, does not refer to eternity in a philosophical sense but has the sense of durability or "long-lastingness." Dtr is not clear about the fulfillment of this prophecy. On the one hand, Solomon refers to his succession of his father as the fulfillment of Yahweh's promise to David (1 Kgs 8:20, 24-25). On the other hand, 1 Kgs 15:4 and 2 Kgs 8:19, which explain Yahweh's refusal to destroy Judah because of his promise to David, suggest that the promise is still operative and being fulfilled. The promise might be seen as fulfilled in the fact that the dynasty endured for such a long time. However, Dtr is completely silent about this and especially about how the promise is to be interpreted in the shadow of the exile. In any case, the Davidic promise accounts for the endurance of the dynasty and the kingdom of Judah beyond Israel.

Another prophet, Ahijah, actually offers the same opportunity for an enduring dynasty to Jeroboam (1 Kgs 11:31-39) if he, like David, will remain faithful. Jeroboam, however, commits apostasy by building the shrines at

Dan and Bethel (12:26-33), and each king of Israel after him perpetuates this sin by maintaining those two shrines. Thus, the two contrasting themes of the promise to David and the sin of Jeroboam function together etiologically in Kings to explain the contrasting royal histories of Israel and Judah — a series of coups and dynasties in Israel as opposed to a single dynasty in Judah that continued as a kingdom for well over a century beyond Israel's end.

Challenges in Reading Kings

History

The book of Kings presents several distinct challenges to its readers and interpreters, especially those who may be approaching it in a careful way for the first time. To begin, there is the matter of how to balance the book's sometimes competing interests in theology and history. The etiological purpose suggested by King's structure indicates that its prime concerns are probably more theological than historical, if the latter means detailing what happened in the past. This accords with the understanding of ancient history writing as discussed in Chapter One above. It is also indicated by the fact that the kings of Israel and Judah are evaluated not on their social, political, or military accomplishments but on religious grounds. Furthermore, prophets, more than kings, are the heroes of the book and the ones who set, or at least announce, the direction of history.

Perhaps the best illustration of the book's nature is found in its handling of King Omri of Israel. Historically and politically, Omri was an important king — perhaps, in fact, the most important of all the kings of Israel. We know this from the archaeological, especially architectural, remains from his reign and from the fact that Assyrian inscriptions refer to Israel as "the house of Omri" long after his reign had ended. However, outside of the account of the civil war by which he came to power and the customary regnal formulas, the book of Kings has only a single verse about Omri's reign, and it is merely a description of Omri's purchase and fortification of Samaria (1 Kgs 16:24). By contrast, there are six chapters in Kings about Omri's son, Ahab (16:29–22:40). Now, Ahab was also an important king in his own right, though certainly no more so than his father. The disparity is due not to historical factors but to religious ones — specifically, Ahab's marriage to the foreign, Baal-worshipping Jezebel and the opposition to them by the prophet Elijah.

Kings' overriding theological interests pose a problem when it comes to using the book for historical purposes. It should be understood, first of all, that the book of Kings, practically, is our only real source of information for the monarchical history of Israel and Judah. As we will see shortly, the Bible's other history of the period, 2 Chronicles, is essentially an interpretation of Kings and not an independent record. The prophetic books contain only a sprinkling of names and allusions to events that would be of little use without the sequential register of names and events in the book of Kings. Outside of the Bible, archaeology sheds light on the cultural practices and institutions mentioned in the Bible, but it does not usually provide the sort of details about specific individuals and events furnished by the Kings narrative. Assyrian and Babylonian inscriptions yield only a handful of names of kings of Israel and Judah and virtually no information about their reigns.

The relationship of the Kings narrative to history is something of an open question. On the one hand, the book contains a good deal of history. This is clear from the historical confirmation through inscriptions or archaeological artifacts of a number of the characters and events to which Kings refers. Cited, in chronological order, are some well-known examples:

- Pharaoh Sheshonq's (Shishak) relief on the wall of the Amun temple in Thebes celebrates his raid into Canaan mentioned in 1 Kgs 14:25-26.
- The recently discovered Aramaic stela fragments from Tel Dan that mention the "house of David" also contain the names Ahaziah of Judah and Jehoram of Israel, the author taking the credit for their deaths, which the Bible assigns to Jehu (2 Kings 9–10).
- The "Mesha stela" from the Moabite king of that name (2 Kgs 3:4-27) also refers to Omri of Israel.
- The Assyrian account of the battle of Qarqar (853 B.C.E.) mentions King Ahab of Israel as a leading member of the coalition opposed to Shalmaneser III.
- The "Black Obelisk" depicts "Yahua, son of Omri," probably Jehu, bowing down before the same Shalmaneser III.
- The annals of Sennacherib describe Hezekiah and the Assyrian siege

of Jerusalem in 701, and a relief from the Assyrian king's palace in Nineveh depicts the siege and capture of the Judahite fortress of Lachish.

- The Siloam tunnel inscription, though it does not contain Hezekiah's name, describes the hewing out of the water conduit that he commissioned in anticipation of an Assyrian siege of Jerusalem (2 Kgs 20:20).
- The Babylonian Chronicle of Nebuchadrezzar II recounts the capture of Jerusalem in 597.

On the other hand, the book of Kings also contains historical inaccuracies or problems that complicate its use for historical reconstruction. These are of several kinds. One kind has to do with contradictions and problems in the numerous chronological data contained in the book. This is a complicated issue and merits its own discussion (below).

Another kind of problem concerns information given in Kings that does not square with what is otherwise known. A prime example is the prophetic stories in 1 Kings 20 and 22.[2] The stories are placed within the reign of Ahab, and in both cases he is specifically named as the Israelite king. However, as scholars have long observed, the description of the king of Israel in these stories does not match well with what is known about Ahab and his reign elsewhere in biblical and extrabiblical sources. For instance, Assyrian inscriptions from the ninth century describe an enemy coalition in which Ahab is a powerful ally of Aram (Syria). This portrait clashes with the one in 1 Kings 20 and 22 both in terms of the animosity they describe between Israel and Aram and the weakness attributed to Israel. There are also internal problems suggesting that the stories are out of place. For instance, the Israelite king in 1 Kings 22 dies in battle. This conflicts with Ahab's closing formula, which says that he "slept with his fathers" (22:40), a statement that occurs elsewhere only for kings who die peacefully. These tensions have led many scholars to conclude that the biblical stories are better suited to and originally concerned a king in the later Jehu dynasty, either Jehoahaz or Joash. As I will suggest below, the two chapters are part of a group of prophetic tales that were added to Kings at a post-Dtr stage, causing historical and literary difficulties.

2. For a more detailed discussion of these chapters and bibliography, see McKenzie, *The Trouble with Kings*, 88-93.

A similar kind of historical problem in which theological factors play a role along with literary ones is Kings' mention of two invasions by the Assyrian king Sennacherib during Hezekiah's reign (2 Kgs 18:13-16; 18:17–19:37).[3] The most likely and most widely held viewpoint is that the two accounts in Kings are different versions of the same invasion — one that took place in 701 B.C.E. — and that Sennacherib's annals relate the same event in terms somewhat similar to the first version in Kings. The second version is probably Dtr's composition, and it was introduced for theological reasons. Its focus is on religious matters such as Hezekiah's trust in Yahweh, Yahweh's loyalty to the Davidic promise, and Sennacherib's blasphemy against Yahweh, all of which lead Yahweh to send an angel to strike the Assyrian camp, resulting in Sennacherib's return home (where he is ignominiously assassinated by two of his sons) and the salvation of Jerusalem. It is impossible to know the historical reason for Sennacherib's withdrawal. It may be that some kind of disaster, such as disease in his army, compelled him to lift his siege of Jerusalem prematurely. But this is speculation. What does seem clear is that Jerusalem's survival, whatever the reasons for it, inspired Dtr's theological enhancement of the story, thus producing the account in the Bible. It is also evident that Dtr here "telescopes" historical events for theological reasons. Sennacherib's assassination occurred in and had nothing to do with his invasion of Judah, which had taken place twenty years earlier. Historically, the two events were unrelated, but Kings draws them together for theological reasons.

Such inaccuracies and problems do not disqualify the book of Kings as a historical source. But they do show that it has to be used judiciously, no less than any ancient literary source, for historical reconstruction. In the first place, certain stories, such as those about the wonder-working "men of God" from Israel should probably be regarded as purely legendary. Others, however, may be weighed to separate theology from history. The prophecy-fulfillment scheme discussed above furnishes a good example. Dtr's use of this scheme to account etiologically and theologically for the series of overthrows of royal houses in Israel indicates that the basic portrait of Israel's monarchy as a succession of dynasties is historically accurate. Using the same line of reasoning, in 1 Kings 11–12 there are two distinct reasons given for the division of Israel and Judah — Solomon's apostasies and the oppression of the northern tribes by the Davidic house.

3. Again, see McKenzie, *The Trouble with Kings*, 103-7.

Since the former was Dtr's way of accounting theologically for the event, the latter, involving Solomon's labor force and the provincial system that it supported (1 Kgs 4:7-19), may have a basis in history.

Chronology

In general, the regnal formulas in Kings and the data they contain would seem to provide the kind of information useful for historical reconstruction, at least for the chronological skeleton of the monarchies of Israel and Judah. There are actually two kinds of chronology in play here — relative and absolute. The dates in Kings represent a relative chronology, since the kings of Israel and Judah are dated relative to one another. Absolute dates are the numbers for years B.C.E. These are based on the records of other kingdoms, particularly Egypt, Assyria, and Babylonia, correlated with recorded, datable astronomical phenomena, such as eclipses. Some absolute dates provide chronological pegs around which the dating of events and characters in Kings are built. These pegs include:

- Pharaoh Sheshonq's (Shishak's) invasion of Judah — ca. 925
- The battle of Qarqar, in which King Ahab of Israel participated — 853
- The fall of Samaria to Shalmaneser V of Assyria — 722/721
- The invasion of Sennacherib — 701
- The capture of Jerusalem by the Babylonians — March 15/16, 597

Chronological reconstruction entails correlating the relative chronological information in Kings to absolute dates established by these pegs. This would seem on the surface to be a more-or-less simple process. The difficulties involved in carrying it out, however, quickly become apparent when one examines the figures in Kings. These figures are not in agreement with each other or with external dates, and Kings sometimes even includes multiple and variant regnal numbers for the same king. The figures for the Omride dynasty are particularly vexing. Consider the following problems inherent in the figures for this period.

- The beginning of Omri's twelve-year reign is dated to the thirty-first year of Asa of Judah (1 Kgs 16:23). But the start of the reign of Omri's son Ahab is placed at Asa's thirty-eighth year (16:29), which would give Omri only a seven-year reign. If Asa reigned forty-one years as 1 Kgs 15:10 states, then a twelve-year reign for Omri would mean that he died one to two years after Asa.

- Jehoram of Israel is said to have begun his reign in the second year of Jehoram of Judah in 2 Kgs 1:17, but in the eighteenth year of Jehoshaphat, Jehoram's father, according to 2 Kgs 3:1.

- The start of Ahaziah's reign over Judah is placed in both the eleventh and twelfth year of Joram of Israel (2 Kgs 8:25; 9:29).

Not surprisingly, in view of these kinds of individual problems, Kings' figures for the two kingdoms do not agree. The total number of years of the Israelite kings from Jeroboam to Jehu's revolt is 98, while the number for Judahite kings for the same period is 95. Similarly, the total for Israelite kings from Jehu to the end of the kingdom is 143 years and seven months, while the figures for Judahite kings during the same period total 165 years.

What is more, the relative dating in Kings collides at points with the absolute pegs listed above. Such is the case for Hezekiah, who is said to have begun his reign in the third year of Hoshea (2 Kgs 18:1), who in turn reigned nine years until the fall of Samaria in 722/721 (17:1-6). These dates, therefore, presuppose that Hezekiah took the throne in 728/727. But 2 Kgs 18:13 dates Sennacherib's invasion of 701 to Hezekiah's fourteenth year, yielding a date of 715 as the latter's accession year.

Apart from simply regarding the entire chronological system and all of the figures in it as artificial — a position adopted by some scholars — two basic solutions to these problems have been proposed. One solution assumes that the chronology represented in the Hebrew text (MT) is essentially correct and that the numbers can be harmonized and explained.[4] This explanation involves postulating co-regencies and interregna in certain cases. In addition, the use of different calendars based on fall or spring new years is presumed as operating in Israel and Judah and/or in different periods. Another theory is that different systems were used for reckoning the start of a king's reign from the new year just before the king's accession (an-

---

4. This view is most widely associated with Edwin R. Thiele, *The Mysterious Numbers of the Hebrew Kings: A Reconstruction of the Chronology of the Kingdoms of Israel and Judah* (Chicago: University of Chicago Press, 1951). A comparable approach is adopted in the more recent work by Gershon Galil, *The Chronology of the Kings of Israel and Judah*. Studies in the History and Culture of the Ancient Near East 9 (Leiden: Brill, 1996).

tedating) or from the first new year following his accession (postdating). While some of these factors may have been operational in ancient Israel and Judah, the application of them by modern scholars to solve individual problems often seems arbitrary and reflective of special pleading. Furthermore, it is hard to imagine how the author, Dtr, would have left such diverse numbers from conflicting systems of calculation unreconciled.

The other solution is not really a solution but the recognition that the Old Greek text of Kings contained a different and probably older chronology than the MT, especially for the Omride period.[5] The Old Greek chronology may not be original, and following it does not solve all of the chronological problems in the text. However, it does appear to represent a better starting point for chronological reconstruction than does the MT.[6]

Text

The chronological differences between the LXX and MT in Kings highlight the importance of text-critical factors for the book. The discussion of textual criticism in Chapter Three above described how the Dead Sea Scrolls have shown the variety of textual traditions behind the Hebrew Bible. As we saw in the previous chapter, the book of Samuel was the parade example, since the 4QSam[a] fragments proved to have greater affinity with the LXX text than with the MT. The situation is quite different for the book of Kings, however. For one thing, the Dead Sea Scroll evidence for Kings is sparser and less diverse than it is for Samuel.[7] The LXX is also less diverse

---

5. This was observed independently in two dissertations written in the 1960s: J. Maxwell Miller, "The Omride Dynasty in the Light of Recent Literary and Archaeological Research" (Diss., Emory, 1964); and James Donald Shenkel, *Chronology and Recensional Development in the Greek Text of Kings.* HSM 1 (Cambridge, MA: Harvard University Press, 1968).

6. As recognized in the recent chronological reconstructions by William Hamilton Barnes, *Studies in the Chronology of the Divided Monarchy of Israel.* HSM 48 (Atlanta: Scholars, 1991) and M. Christine Tetley, *The Reconstructed Chronology of the Divided Kingdom* (Winona Lake: Eisenbrauns, 2005).

7. Cave 4, where extensive fragments from three scrolls of Samuel were found, yielded only portions of 1 Kgs 7:20-21, 25-27, 29-42, 50 or 51; 7:51–8:9; 8:16-18. See Julio Trebolle Barrera, "4QKgs," in *Qumran Cave 4.IX,* ed. Eugene C. Ulrich, Frank Moore Cross, et al. *DJD* 14 (1995) 171-83. Cave 5 produced identifiable fragments of 1 Kgs 1:1, 16-17, 27-37 published by J. T. Milik, "Textes de la grotte 5Q: I Rois," in *Les 'Petites Grottes' de Qumrân,* ed. Baillet, J. T. Milik, and R. de Vaux. *DJD* 3 (1962) 171-72. The Kings fragments of Cave 6 included 1 Kgs

in Kings. This is because in Codex Vaticanus (LXX^B), the best representative of the LXX, the oldest available Greek translation (known as the "Old Greek" [OG]) is preserved only in 1 Kgs 2:12–21:29. The rest of the LXX of Kings reflects a first-century c.e. revision of the Greek text toward the developing MT known as the *kaige* recension.[8]

However, where the older Greek version is extant, the situation reflects just as much complexity as in Samuel, since the OG of Kings often differs markedly from the MT. This is especially so in 1 Kings 4–11, where the OG attests a very different arrangement of the material. The OG also reverses the order of 1 Kings 20–21 vis-à-vis the MT, such that the prophetic stories in chs. 20 and 22:1-38 go together. Moreover, there are extensive "supplements" in the LXX at 1 Kgs 2:35; 2:46; and 12:24a-z that were originally made in the Hebrew text, not after its translation into Greek. Their nature is intensely debated among scholars, with some believing them to preserve older source (pre-Dtr) material and others considering them interpretive or midrashic.

Sources

The main sources that have been postulated for Kings are of two kinds — regnal or official and prophetic. The regnal formulas that provide the framework of the book give the impression that the author had access to some kind of official archives for the histories of Israel and Judah. Furthering that impression is the fact that the author refers the reader to three sources for further information about individual kings. These are: the book of the affairs of Solomon (1 Kgs 11:41), the book of the daily affairs of the kings of Israel (1 Kgs 14:19; 15:31; 16:5, 14, 20, 27; 22:39; 2 Kgs 1:18; 10:34; 13:8, 12; 14:15, 28; 15:11, 15, 26, 31), and the book of the daily affairs of the kings of Judah (1 Kgs 14:29; 15:7, 23; 22:45; 2 Kgs 8:23; 12:19; 14:18; 15:6, 36; 16:19; 20:20; 21:17, 25; 23:28; 24:5). The usual understanding of these three "books" as official records of some kind, such as court annals, seems reasonable, especially in view of certain details provided for the kings, such as the lengths of their

---

3:12-14; 12:28-31; 22:28-31; 2 Kgs 5:26; 6:32; 7:8-10; 7:20–8:5; 9:1-2; 10:19-21 as published by M. Baillet, "Grotte 6: Livres des Rois," in Baillet, Milik, and de Vaux, *DJD* 3 (1962) 107-12.

8. Where the OG is not extant, its variants can sometimes be perceived in manuscripts of the Lucianic type (LXX^L), the older stratum of which is an ancient text form known as the "proto–Lucianic" text, which approximates the OG.

reigns, names of the mothers of most of the kings of Judah, and specifics about their activities. Moreover, such annals are well known for other ancient Near Eastern, particularly Assyrian and Babylonian, kings.

Still, further considerations call for caution. First, no official documents or court annals of this nature outside of the Bible have been discovered for any Israelite or Judean king. Second, in addition to the kinds of details one would expect to derive from royal annals, such as the number of years of a king's reign, the regnal formulas also give religious evaluations for the kings. The evaluations are patently Dtr and would hardly be encountered in an annalistic document. Finally, there are differences or changes within the formulas, such as the presence or absence of the queen mother's name and the presence or absence of a location for the king's burial. These changes have been taken by some scholars as reflecting different annalistic source documents and/or redactional levels.[9] But no single explanation for the changes has yet achieved consensus. The changes are noteworthy, but it is not clear that they stem from different official documents. They do not match with the three sources cited by the author of Kings, so that attributing them to such annalistic sources in a sense undercuts the author's claim to have used such documents. To put it in a slightly different way, the idea that Dtr used annalistic sources is based on the presence of similar "recordlike" data for different kings. But that consideration is undermined to some extent by the differences within the presumed records. In short, while Dtr may have used official records of some sort, their exact nature is unknown and even their existence is uncertain.

Whatever the source of the regnal formulas, it is clear that they function as the basic narrative skeleton of the book of Kings. That skeleton, though, is infused with stories about prophets, especially prophets from the northern kingdom. Such stories are regularly integrated within the ac-

---

9. The most influential such theory has been that of Helga Weippert in "Die 'deuteronomistischen' Beurteilung der Könige von Israel und Juda und das Problem der Redaktion der Königsbücher," *Bib* 53 (1972) 301-39. A similar, more detailed study is that of Baruch Halpern and David S. Vanderhooft, "The Editions of Kings in the 7th-6th Centuries B.C.E.," *HUCA* 62 (1991) 179-244. A slightly different focus is adopted by Iain W. Provan, *Hezekiah and the Book of Kings: A Contribution to the Debate About the Composition of the Deuteronomistic History.* BZAW 172 (Berlin: de Gruyter, 1988). He detects two different understandings of the "high places" *(bāmôt)* in the regnal formulas of the kings of Judah and suggests that they betray two different editions of the DtrH, the first climaxing with Hezekiah's reign and the second exilic.

counts of the Israelite kings to whom the prophets relate. This has led to the suggestion that Dtr made use of one or more collections of prophetic tales and or even an extended, pre-Dtr narrative about prophets.[10] The question of the existence and nature of such documents, however, is complicated by several considerations.

For example, the prophetic stories do not all appear at the same level of writing. That is, some are well integrated into the Dtr framework and narrative while others are not, and the latter therefore appear to be post-Dtr additions to the book. Two examples of prophetic stories that are well integrated into the DtrH are 1 Kgs 14:1-14 and 2 Kgs 9:1-10. In 1 Kgs 14:1-14, Jeroboam sends his wife to inquire of the prophet Ahijah whether their sick son will recover from his illness. Though she is disguised, Ahijah knows who she is when he hears the sound of her feet (v. 6), and he tells her to go home, that when her feet enter the city the boy will die (v. 12). But his announcement is interrupted by a prediction of the destruction of the royal house in distinctly Dtr language (vv. 7-11). In other words, Dtr used an older story about the prophet's prediction of the death of Jeroboam's son as a template for the insertion of an oracle against Jeroboam's line. In so doing, he changed the story from a tale about Ahijah's powers as a "man of God" to one of his prophecies against a northern royal house.

This same kind of alteration of an older prophetic story is even more apparent in another example from the narrative about Jehu's revolt, this time involving the prophet Elisha. In 2 Kgs 9:1-3 Elisha appoints a trainee of his to go to the town of Ramoth-gilead, where the Israelite army is camped for war against the Syrians. Elisha's orders are quite explicit. The young prophet is to take the general, Jehu, into a private room, anoint him as king, and then leave immediately; he is not to dally. Stories about prophets elsewhere in Kings make clear that precise obedience to such orders is crucial, since disobedience can bring death (cf. 1 Kings 13). It is surprising, therefore, that the trainee diverges from Elisha's instructions. Instead of fleeing immediately after anointing Jehu, he delivers an oracle commanding Jehu to annihilate the house of Ahab (2 Kgs 9:7-10a). It is another Dtr prophecy against a royal house, this time Omri's/Ahab's. Once again, Dtr

---

10. So Antony F. Campbell's theory of an early "Prophetic Record" in *Of Prophets and Kings: A Late Ninth Century Document (1 Samuel 1–2 Kings 10).* CBQMS 17 (Washington: Catholic Biblical Association, 1986) and Campbell and Mark A. O'Brien, *Unfolding the Deuteronomistic History: Origins, Upgrades, Present Text* (Minneapolis: Fortress, 2000).

has used an older prophetic story as the setting for one of his prophecies against the northern dynasties, which, as we have seen, are the backbone to his narrative scheme in Kings.

In contrast to these two examples, the story of Elisha's succession of Elijah in 2 Kings 2 is not integrated within the Dtr framework. It is not situated within the reign of any Israelite king but falls in the "crack" between the report of the death of Ahaziah (2 Kgs 1:17-18) and the formula for the accession of Jehoram (3:1-3). Similarly, the report of Elisha's death (2 Kgs 13:14-25) follows the closing formula for King Jehoash of Israel (13:12-13).[11] The fact that these two stories were not integrated into the framework suggests that they were post-Dtr additions to the book of Kings.

Even some prophetic stories that were properly placed within the framework of the regnal formulas were likely post-Dtr additions. Source-critical analysis suggests that most of the Elijah (1 Kings 17–19 + 2 Kgs 1:2-17aα) and Elisha stories (2 Kings 2; 3:4-27; 4:1–8:15; 13:14-21) as well as those in 1 Kings 13; 20; and 22:1-38 are post-Dtr additions to the book rather than source material used by Dtr.[12] These stories exhibit a lack of Dtr language or reworking that would indicate their actual incorporation into the Dtr level of Kings, and their view of the prophets as wonder-working "men of God" contrasts with the role of prophets elsewhere in the DtrH simply as conveyors of the divine word. In the case of 1 Kings 13, the specific reference to Josiah by name some three hundred years before his reign is unusual. Here, the technique of narrative resumption *(Wiederaufnahme)* has been used to insert the story into a preexisting narrative. In this technique, some material from the text into which an insertion is made is reiterated after the insertion so as to take it up at the point where it was dissected.[13]

Theology

The basic reason for the condemnation of Jeroboam and the kings of the north was that by building and maintaining the national shrines at Dan

---

11. The repetition of the formula in 14:15-16 is secondary as indicated by its occurrence at the end of a story about the Judahite king and by the absence of v. 15 from the LXX[L], the best witness to the OG in this section of Kings.

12. For details, see McKenzie, *The Trouble with Kings*, 81-100.

13. Cf. 12:32 and 13:33, and see the discussion in McKenzie, *The Trouble with Kings*, 51-56.

and Bethel they violated the principle of centralization. This is the Dtr doctrine that there is only one place where worship of Yahweh can legitimately be conducted, namely, the temple in Jerusalem. Dtr's application of the principle of centralization to Jeroboam was anachronistic. That is, the doctrine of centralization was not in existence in Jeroboam's time. It first appears in the Bible in the book of Deuteronomy, which was written in the late seventh century B.C.E., and it was probably an invention associated with King Josiah's political and religious reform movement.

According to 2 Kings 22, the "book of the law" was discovered while cleaning out the temple in Josiah's eighteenth year (622). This was a common device used by kings in antiquity to legitimate programs they wished to undertake, so that the lawbook was probably actually written at this time. Correlations between the reforms instituted by Josiah on the basis of that book as described in 2 Kings 23 have long led scholars to identify it as some form of the book of Deuteronomy. Thus, Deuteronomy in its original edition was probably written in support of Josiah's reforms. Part of what Josiah sought to do was to consolidate the kingdom religiously and politically under his central administration in Jerusalem as a strategy of resistance against the Assyrian Empire. The promotion of centralization in Deuteronomy was a part of this program. The later author of the DtrH adopted it, explaining the fall of Israel as a result of the violation of this principle by Jeroboam and his successors.

Dtr used the principle of centralization to bookend his work in the DtrH. In the book of Kings, Jeroboam's transgression of centralization is preceded by Solomon's construction of the temple (1 Kings 5–7), which places the transgression in high relief. At the other end of the work, Deut 12:1-7 promises that Yahweh will choose "the place" that will be designated for cultic worship. Solomon fulfills that promise by building the temple in Jerusalem. Thus, the construction and use of the northern shrines flew in the face of the will and plan of Yahweh. From the perspective of the northern kings and their contemporaries, the building and maintenance of national shrines was the proper form of devotion. But since Israel was destroyed by Assyria in 721 B.C.E., they were not around to offer a counterpoint to Deuteronomy's centralization in 622 or its later development by Dtr.

Not surprisingly, the theology of Kings corresponds with that of Deuteronomy in other respects that are related to the centralization doctrine. For instance, there is the idea of divine election embodied in the choice of Jerusalem and of the Davidic dynasty, expressed in the promise to David, and carried through the monarchy of Judah in the book of Kings. The endurance of Judah and the Davidic monarchy demonstrate Yahweh's faithfulness to his promise. In Deuteronomy, Israel is also God's elect among the nations. That election is applied through the Davidic dynasty to Judah, as stressed in the book of Kings, above all in Solomon's prayer at the dedication of the temple (1 Kings 8), where Solomon constantly refers to Israel as Yahweh's people and bases his petitions for God's continuing faithfulness and mercy upon their election.

Solomon's prayer acknowledges that Israel will not always fulfill the responsibility that election as God's people implies. The story of the book of Kings is one of failure. The kings and people of Israel and Judah are responsible for keeping the law prescribed in Deuteronomy. A corollary is the idea of Scripture. Whether the "book of the law" was really (re)discovered by Josiah's workers or was actually commissioned by him, it furnishes one of the earliest, if not the earliest example in Israel's history of Scripture as a written guide for cultic and religious activity.

One of the closest areas of affiliation between Deuteronomy and Kings concerns the related notions of punishment for sin and reward for obedience. Deuteronomy envisions Israel's destruction if it disobeys the law, and this vision is fulfilled in Kings. This dimension of Dtr's theology is often referred to as "prophetic," and indeed it resembles the theology of those books of the Latter Prophets in the Hebrew Bible that call on their audience to repent by threatening destruction. In Kings, the northern kingdom is destroyed because of its disobedience (2 Kings 17). Then Judah falls to the Babylonians for much the same reason (2 Kings 24–25). The fact that Judah falls after Josiah's successful reforms almost makes destruction seem inevitable. The book of Kings as it stands blames this on Manasseh and to a lesser extent on the trajectory set by previous kings. This rather contrived explanation has even led many scholars to suspect that an initial, positively oriented edition of the DtrH promoting Josiah's reform was written during his reign but had to be revised due to the less-than-positive turn of events.[14]

The idea that Yahweh is Israel's God exclusively is fundamental to all

14. For a treatment of this matter and a defense of the unity of the DtrH on this point, see Percy S. F. van Keulen, *Manasseh Through the Eyes of the Deuteronomists: The Manasseh Account (2 Kings 21:1-18) and the Final Chapters of the Deuteronomistic History*. OtSt 38 (Leiden: Brill, 1996).

of the other concepts we have been surveying. Deuteronomy is often described as being on the "threshold" of monotheism, and the same seems to be true of Kings. Israel and Judah are to worship no other god except Yahweh, and the violation of this principle is one of the chief causes of disaster. Apostasy lies behind the Davidic line's loss of the northern tribes after Solomon (1 Kings 11). Even though the calves and sanctuaries at Dan and Bethel seem to be devoted to Yahweh, Dtr implies that they are not when he has Jeroboam refer to the gods (plural) who brought Israel out of Egypt (1 Kgs 12:28). Jezebel's importation of Baal worship is the main reason for Dtr's hatred of her and for Ahab being viewed as Israel's worst king (1 Kgs 16:31-33). Jehu is praised for his assassination of Jezebel and the bloody coup that ends the Omri dynasty (2 Kings 10), in contrast to Hosea's view of the event as bloody and sinful (Hos 1:4-5). As Kings now stands, the worship of other gods is the main reason for the fall of both Israel (2 Kgs 17:7-18) and Judah (21:1-9).

All of these doctrines and the book of Kings as a whole also assume that Yahweh is in control of history. The tales about prophets attest his control of other nations as well, and of the forces of nature. Other gods are powerless (1 Kings 18), if they even exist. Yahweh is intimately concerned with and involved in the daily activities of his people, both cultic and juridical (1 Kings 21). While it is worth noting that many of the prophetic stories are probably later additions to Dtr's work (see below), the notion of Yahweh as both transcendent and immanent is also emphasized in Solomon's speech at the dedication of the temple (1 Kgs 8:27), a Dtr composition.

It is unclear what vision of the future is held by the author of Kings. The book's focus on the past and virtual silence about the future is its greatest mystery and greatest challenge for interpreters. Will Yahweh restore Israel through Judah and the line of David, or is Israel's end final? The book does not answer this question; at best it offers only vague possibilities about what may happen next. Are the observable patterns of divine and human activity in the past merely pointed out for academic reasons or are they intended as examples and paradigms for future human behavior and grounds for hope in divine response? It seems odd that a writer should compose an extensive work of national history only to explain how and why it all came to a disastrous end. Yet Kings and the DtrH remain strangely silent about the future. No hope or direction for national restoration is clearly expressed or implied. Some scholars propose that the DtrH is "crisis literature," in which the account of the past also provides a foundation myth for the future.[15] Perhaps, then, the point is that the future is open and that knowledge of the past is the best way to prepare for the uncertain future. The future is in Yahweh's hands; all that the remnant of Israel can do is hope that Yahweh will act, as he did in the past, to redeem them, and if he does, to learn from the past and not make the same mistakes of apostasy and disobedience to the law again.

15. See Thomas Römer, *The So-Called Deuteronomistic History: A Sociological, Historical, and Literary Introduction* (London: T&T Clark, 2005) 163-64.

8

1-2 Chronicles

We may begin the treatment of Chronicles by reviewing and enlarging on some points of introduction from Chapter Two above. Like 1-2 Samuel and 1-2 Kings, 1-2 Chronicles are two parts or "volumes" of a single book. The identity of its author is unknown, and he is typically known simply as the Chronicler. I say "he" because the author was likely male, judging from the emphasis that the work places on the role of male religious personnel, especially the priests and Levites, and from what is known of ancient Near Eastern society, in which literacy was restricted for the most part to upper-class males. The Chronicler was an individual author rather than a "school" or group of writers. He was an editor to the extent that he exercised the editorial function of an author using sources. However, his work did not consist merely in editing previous material but in using such material to create a new work. He most likely lived and wrote in the fourth century B.C.E. Most scholars today think that he was distinct from the author of Ezra-Nehemiah, though the two works are linked editorially. The Chronicler probably wrote after Ezra-Nehemiah and perhaps even in response to it. His work in Chronicles is best characterized as history writing, albeit for theological and didactic purposes.

Content and Structure

The book of 1-2 Chronicles is composed of three large sections:

1 Chronicles 1–9	Genealogies of the tribes of Israel
1 Chronicles 10–2 Chronicles 9	Reigns of David and Solomon
2 Chronicles 10–36	Kingdom of Judah

Each of these sections is well organized, the first by tribe, the last by king. The middle section also falls neatly into three parts:

1 Chronicles 10–21	Reign of David
1 Chronicles 22–29	Transition from David to Solomon
2 Chronicles 1–9	Reign of Solomon

As suggested by this division, the reigns of David and Solomon balance and complement each other as two parts of a single era. Together, their reigns represent the "Golden Age" of Israel in the Chronicler's presentation. Solomon brings to fruition the initiatives begun by David, particularly in regard to the building of the temple. Their joint centrality in Israel's history is signaled by their central place in the Chronicler's account.

Sources

Canonical

The time period covered by the narrative portions of Chronicles (i.e., excepting the genealogies in 1 Chronicles 1–9) is the same as that covered by 2 Samuel–2 Kings, namely the reigns of David and Solomon and the history of the subsequent kingdom of Judah. The overlap consists of more than simply covering the same period. The similarity in narrative content of Chronicles in comparison to Samuel–Kings is illustrated in the following chart, where // stands for "parallel to."

1 Chronicles 10–21//1 Samuel 31–2 Samuel 24	David's reign

1 Chronicles 22–29// —	Transition from David to Solomon
2 Chronicles 1–9//1 Kings 1–11	Solomon's reign
2 Chronicles 10–36//1 Kings 12–2 Kings 25	Kingdom of Judah

Thus, except for the genealogies in 1 Chronicles 1–9 and the transitional section in 1 Chronicles 22–29, Chronicles basically reiterates and often virtually repeats the parallel material in Samuel-Kings.

The fact that Chronicles so obviously and so closely follows the material in Samuel and Kings is the main reason its genre is sometimes designated as "rewritten Bible."[1] But Samuel-Kings are not the only canonical writings used by the Chronicler. The genealogies draw from Genesis, Exodus, Numbers, Joshua, and perhaps Ruth, in addition to Samuel, and 1 Chr 9:2-17a probably borrows its list of residents of Jerusalem from Neh 11:3-19. Chronicles' narrative attests familiarity with the legal material in Exodus, Numbers, Leviticus, and Deuteronomy. There are allusions to Isaiah, Jeremiah, Zechariah, and Malachi, at least, among the prophets, and citations from the Psalms (esp. 1 Chronicles 16).

The close similarity of Chronicles to Samuel-Kings has received a great deal of attention from scholars, and rightly so, for it is the only instance in the Bible where we have both an extended literary work and its principal source. We can get a clearer picture than anywhere else of how one biblical writer made use of his sources through supplementation, abbreviation, and adaptation. These changes provide insight into the Chronicler's ideological interests and motives and how they shaped his literary activity. Studying Chronicles in close comparison with Samuel-Kings yields a clearer sense than anywhere else in the Bible of how its authors worked, how much freedom they could feel to shape their work, and by contrast what limits may have restricted them. For readers new to Chronicles, this is the way to begin — with a close comparison to Samuel-Kings. It will be the focus of our treatment to follow. Readers who are unfamiliar with Chronicles may be surprised at first by the number and extent of the changes effected by the Chronicler reflecting the relative freedom he apparently felt to exercise creativity in the service of ideology.

---

1. For a discussion and characterization of this genre, see Sidnie White Crawford, *Rewriting Scripture in Second Temple Times*. SDSSRL (Grand Rapids: Wm. B. Eerdmans, 2008) 1-18.

While the value of this approach to Chronicles — close reading in comparison with Samuel-Kings — can hardly be overstated, it must be tempered by three considerations. First, the Chronicler may not have expected his audience to make the kind of close comparison with Samuel-Kings that modern readers make, given that literacy was less common and books much less readily available than today. The Chronicler seems to have anticipated general familiarity with Samuel-Kings on the part of his readers (cf. 1 Chr 10:13-14), but not necessarily detailed knowledge. In fact, his anticipation of only *general* familiarity may have contributed to his sense of freedom in reshaping the stories and especially in changing some of the details in them to suit his purposes.

Second, the text of Samuel-Kings used by the Chronicler was not the same as that preserved in the Hebrew Bible. As discussed in Chapter Two above, the Dead Sea Scrolls showed that a variety of texts of the books of the Bible existed at the turn of the eras. In parallel passages, Chronicles attests greater affinity with the principal Dead Sea Scrolls manuscript of Samuel (4QSam^a) and the LXX of Samuel than with the MT of Samuel.[2] This means the Chronicler cannot be assumed to be responsible for all of the differences between the Hebrew texts of Samuel-Kings and Chronicles. Unfortunately, 4QSam^a is fragmentary, so that evidence of a variant reading is not always available. But it is a possibility that must be borne in mind whenever one suspects deliberate change on the Chronicler's part.

Third, whatever its similarities to and differences with Samuel-Kings, Chronicles must also be read as a literary and theological work in its own right. The Chronicler did much more than simply repeat what was in his canonical sources. Those sources were only a beginning point, the basic data or traditions with which he worked. The process by which he interpreted and expounded on these sources was sophisticated and creative. It has been shown, for example, that the Chronicler made use of a number of literary and exegetical techniques present in later Judaism that were not necessarily ideologically driven.[3] Chronicles, in short, is an original work with its own set of messages and ideas, but also its own literary beauty and complexity. Readers of Chronicles will do well, therefore, to be attuned to

2. This was shown by Werner E. Lemke, "Synoptic Studies in the Chronicler's History" (diss., Harvard, 1963); and "The Synoptic Problem in the Chronicler's History," *HTR* 58 (1965) 349-63.

3. Isaac Kalimi, *The Reshaping of Ancient Israelite History in Chronicles* (Winona Lake: Eisenbrauns, 2005).

the themes that surface in the work and the creative way that the Chronicler uses them, quite apart from their presence or absence in Samuel-Kings.

As suggested by the reference above to supplementation, abbreviation, and adaptation, the Chronicler's changes in relation to Samuel-Kings might be classed in three categories: additions, omissions, and alterations. In the category of *additions*, the blocks in 1 Chronicles 1–9 and 22–29 have already been noted. The genealogies in the first nine chapters serve to introduce the work on several levels. Literarily, they stand at the head of the narrative, thereby signaling their importance. Historically, they summarize Israel's history at least until David and perhaps, proleptically, for its entire national existence. Theologically, they highlight Israel's self identity (see below on the "all Israel" motif); their internal arrangement also indicates which tribes the Chronicler deems to be of greatest significance. Chapters 22–29 contain a variety of materials (lists, speeches, prayers, as well as some narratives) that are focused on David's preparation of the materials and personnel for building the temple, a task with which Solomon is charged. In addition to these two large blocks, there are other, briefer additions in Chronicles. Whether they come in the form of speeches, prayers, or narratives, they are particularly rich sources for discerning the Chronicler's ideological interests and messages as well as his authorial style and literary expertise.

The most striking *omissions* are again those that concern large blocks of material. Assuming that the Chronicler omits material he cannot accommodate to his interests and message, these omissions are telling for what those interests seem to be. He leaves out practically everything about Saul, narrating only his death as a way of clearing the road for David's advent (1 Chronicles 10). He also omits the stories of David's affair with Bathsheba (most of 2 Samuel 11–12) and Absalom's revolt (2 Samuel 13–20), presumably because these episodes reflect negatively on David's image. Similarly, the judgment upon Solomon for worshiping the gods of his foreign wives (1 Kings 11) is lacking in Chronicles. Additionally, all of the material from the book of Kings that deals with the northern kingdom of Israel is gone from Chronicles, except where such material is pertinent to Judah. These omissions indicate the Chronicler's positive orientation toward David and Solomon and the tribe and kingdom of Judah, as we will see, because it houses the temple. The Chronicler's attitude toward the north is a more complicated question that will be treated shortly.

Alteration is a catchall term for all other changes introduced by the Chronicler. As already suggested, it can be difficult to determine where the Chronicler has changed his source as well as the reason for the change. This category includes rearrangements that the Chronicler has made in his source, such as his transfer of lists and stories of David's "mighty men" (2 Sam 23:8–39) to the setting of David's coronation (1 Chr 11:10-47). There are several instances in 2 Chronicles where the evaluation of a king found in Kings is reversed or where the king's reign is organized into distinct periods of good and evil. The reason for these changes is usually described as the Chronicler's doctrine of "immediate retribution/reward," which is discussed below.

Noncanonical

There are two questions regarding the Chronicler's noncanonical sources: the nature of the sources he cites and whether there were other sources used but not cited. Chronicles contains two kinds of source citations: references to official documents of some kind (e.g., "the book of the kings of Israel and Judah") and references to prophetic sources. The former probably constitute a different way of referring to the book of Kings rather than a reference to independent sources. One reason for this conclusion is that they occur in Chronicles in the same place where there are source citations in Kings, even when that is not the end of Chronicles' account for a particular king. The artificiality of the prophetic sources is indicated by 2 Chr 9:29, which refers to three prophetic records where 1 Kgs 11:41 mentions "the book of the acts of Solomon," even though everything in 2 Chronicles 9 appears to be drawn from Kings and no other source. In both cases, the citation of sources in Chronicles seems to be a literary strategy imitating Kings and lending authenticity to the Chronicles narrative.

At the same time, the Chronicler does appear to have used sources that he does not explicitly cite. Additional information not found in Kings but historically verifiable could have come from oral tradition or common local knowledge rather than writing. The reference to Hezekiah's tunnel in 2 Chr 32:30 might be explained this way, as could the correction of 2 Kgs 23:29 in 2 Chr 35:20 to the effect that Pharaoh Neco went to aid Assyria, not oppose it. Items such as lists of temple personnel and genealogies were likely borrowed from elsewhere rather than invented. However, in many of these cases, the Chronicler appears to have lifted a document from its original setting and placed it in a different context. For instance, archaeological evidence and the locations of the sites suggest that the list of Rehoboam's fortifications (2 Chr 11:5-10) may have originated in Hezekiah's reign two centuries later. Most scholars are skeptical that the Chronicler used additional narrative sources, since the narratives fit so well with the Chronicler's interests and style. It is possible that there was an independent kernel to some such narratives, but if there was, it can no longer be recovered because the Chronicler's rewriting was thorough.

Themes

There are four widely acknowledged themes in Chronicles that represent the book's major theological tenets. These are: the temple and its personnel, the kingship of David and Solomon, the "all Israel" motif, and the so-called doctrine of immediate reward/retribution.

Temple

"Chronicles is really a history of the Jerusalem temple and those who are devoted to it." This characterization of Chronicles by Nelson[4] may be a slight overstatement. But if there is a single main theme to Chronicles, it is certainly the temple, its cult, and its personnel. The temple is crucial to Israel's existence, the heart of its life as a people. It is the Chronicler's central concern and perhaps his main reason for writing. In the postexilic period, following the temple's reconstruction, he seems to be advocating a return to Israel's (idealized) grandeur under David and Solomon through restoring temple worship as he imagines it at that period.

Again to trace the theme, the genealogy of the Levites, as the leading temple personnel, holds pride of place at the center of the genealogies in 1 Chronicles 1–9 and is one of the longest genealogies in those chapters. David's and Solomon's careers revolve around the temple. David's first acts as king are to conquer Jerusalem and bring the ark there (1 Chronicles 13–

---

4. Nelson, *The Historical Books*, 152.

16). As divinely chosen king (ch. 17) he secures the peace of the nation (chs. 18–20) so that the temple may be built and then makes the necessary preparations for its construction (chs. 22–29). Its very blueprint is delivered to David by God (28:19). The Chronicler even risks tarnishing David's ideal reputation by including the story of David's sinful census (1 Chronicles 21) because it ends by designating the spot for the temple's altar. Following David and Solomon, in the rest of 2 Chronicles the kings of Judah are assessed not on political, social, or economic grounds but primarily according to religious critieria, especially their maintenance of proper worship in the temple.

David and Solomon

We have seen that Chronicles presents the reigns of David and Solomon as two phases of a single era, Israel's "Golden Age." The Chronicler idealizes the reigns of both kings, omitting the negative material about them that is contained in Samuel-Kings. The story of David's sin in taking a census is retained (2 Sam 24//1 Chr 21), as noted, evidently because it specifies the location for the altar of the future temple. The retention of this episode illustrates how the careers of David and Solomon in Chronicles revolve around the temple. David conquers Jerusalem, brings the ark into it, and secures the peace and security necessary for Solomon to build the temple. Ironically, the bloodshed required to accomplish the last task disqualifies him from being the temple builder, and that role is left for Solomon. David facilitates his son's work by providing the blueprint and materials for the temple as well as establishing the orders of Levites, gatekeepers, musicians, and other personnel for its day-to-day functioning (1 Chr 22–29).

Because of the focus of the reigns of David and Solomon on activities associated with the temple, some scholars have concluded that the Davidic dynasty in Chronicles is subordinated to the temple and serves only to establish and then maintain temple worship. They suggest, therefore, that the reestablishment of Davidic rule was not a significant element of Chronicles' vision of the ideal past or program for the future. However, the covenant with David granting kingship to him and his line (1 Chronicles 17) is interpreted as a unilateral promise (2 Chr 13:5; 21:7), and those who rebelled against it (i.e., Jeroboam) were guilty of apostasy against Yahweh. While kingship, to be sure, belongs to God, there is no indication in Chronicles that the divine promise was abrogated even by the exile. Davidic rule, in other words, seems to remain an essential element of the Chronicler's vision throughout his work.

All Israel

It was long believed among scholars that the general absence of the history of the northern kingdom of Israel from Chronicles was due to the Chronicler's agreement with the perspective of Ezra-Nehemiah that the northerners had been disinherited by God as part of the chosen people. H. G. M. Williamson's dissertation on "Israel in the Books of Chronicles," published in 1977,[5] demonstrated that the Chronicler's attitude was less monolithic (see Chapter 2 above). True, the northern kingdom was religiously and politically illegitimate from its inception and thus was not afforded a separate narrative history. But the northern people were still part of Yahweh's heritage. Indeed, the Chronicler's ideal vision of the past and for the future is one of all the citizens and tribes of Israel united under the Davidic king.

Tracing this theme through Chronicles, it begins with the genealogies in 1 Chronicles 1–9, which include those for the northern tribes. All Israel takes part in key moments of the nation's early history: the installations of Kings David and Solomon (1 Chr 11:1; 28:1), the conquest of Jerusalem (1 Chr 11:4), transfer of the ark (1 Chr 13:2), and building and dedication of the temple (2 Chr 1:2; 7:8). The Chronicler's slant on the division is expressed in Abijah's speech in 2 Chronicles 13. To be sure, it was an act of rebellion perpetrated against the Davidic dynasty and, by extension, against Yahweh, who had given kingship to David and his heirs. But the rebellion was the act of the one man, Jeroboam, and "certain worthless scoundrels" (13:7 NRSV), who succeeded because of Rehoboam's youth and inexperience. The northerners were led astray, but they remain part of Yahweh's people, and Abijah appeals to them to repent and return to the divinely appointed Davidic rule and the legitimate worship of the Jerusalem temple. Thus, the later king, Hezekiah, is able to restore proper worship for at least some of the northerners (2 Chr 30:1, 25-26; 31:1).

---

5. (Cambridge: Cambridge University Press, 1977).

Immediate Retribution/Reward

The theme of "immediate retribution" has long been recognized by scholars as operating in Chronicles. It first appears in the summary of Saul's reign: "So Saul died for his unfaithfulness. . . . Therefore Yahweh put him to death and turned the kingdom over to David . . ." (1 Chr 10:13-14). The basic idea is that Chronicles presents punishment as forthcoming "immediately," i.e., in a king's lifetime for sinful activity. The title "immediate retribution," however, is misleading, since the principle also incorporates reward for righteous deeds. It therefore is a principle that coincides with the idea of individual responsibility.

The principle is operative especially in 2 Chronicles, as the reigns of the kings of Judah are often divided into "good" and "bad" periods, with righteousness leading to reward followed by sin bringing on punishment, or the other way around. This principle is a tool that the Chronicler exercises in his interpretation of Kings, as certain calamities recorded in the latter are described in Chronicles as divine punishment. It would be wrong, though, to imply that the principle operates mechanically or rigidly, as there is always a chance for repentance — typically signaled by a prophetic warning — and forgiveness, thereby avoiding punishment. In addition, there are disasters narrated in Chronicles that defy easy explanation, and the Chronicler would likely agree that ultimately God's ways are inscrutable to human comprehension.

Supporting Themes

The discussion of these themes has hinted at a number of supporting themes or ideas, and it can be beneficial to the reader of Chronicles to be aware of these in approaching the book. The *rewards* for righteousness mentioned above often come in the form of "quiet" and "rest" for a king's reign as well as military success and strength, a large family, building activities, wealth, and international reputation and are signaled by the Chronicler's use of the verb for "succeed, prosper."

As suggested, *prophets* function particularly in Chronicles to warn wrongdoers of impending punishment in order to effect repentance. Their significance is indicated by 2 Chr 20:20: "Believe in Yahweh your God and you will be established; believe his prophets." The role of prophets is especially clear in the stories about prophets that are without parallel in Samuel-Kings, such that these oracles are almost certainly the Chronicler's composition.

Alongside prophets, *Levites* form an especially important group in Chronicles. This is because the Chronicler ascribes a wide range of roles to them — as temple custodians, gatekeepers, and musicians, but also as scribes and judges. These may have been roles — controversial ones — that the Levites exercised in the Chronicler's own day and that he sought to legitimate by tracing them back to the time of David. The unique portrayal of the Levitical singers in a prophetic role seems especially designed to advocate a cultic capacity for the Levites in the Chronicler's environment.[6]

The extent to which prophets and Levites in Chronicles appeal to written sources (laws, songs, etc.) as opposed to individual inspiration exhibits a growing sense of the authority of *Scripture* in the book. The same development is reflected in the extent to which Chronicles depends on and reiterates information in canonical sources, especially the Pentateuch and Former Prophets.

The Chronicler has sometimes gotten a "bad rap" as a rigid legalist because of his emphasis on proper ritual and obedience to law. But Chronicles also places a great deal of emphasis on *personal attitude*. This is nicely illustrated by the account of Hezekiah's Passover celebration, where allowance is made for individuals who are not ritually clean but whose intentions are right (2 Chr 30:18-20). What is more, Chronicles characterizes proper worship not just as obedient and ritually correct but as joyful and its participants voluntarily generous. This same emphasis on attitude is reflected in other expressions and ideas employed in Chronicles. Thus, disobedience is "rebellion," while the righteous "humble themselves" and "seek" Yahweh. Obedience to legal and ritual prescriptions is merely the means to developing an intimate, personal devotion to God, whose attitude and demeanor toward his people is described by the term "steadfast love" (Hebrew *ḥesed*), which carries the sense of both love and loyalty.

6. David L. Petersen, *Late Israelite Prophecy: Studies in Deutero-Prophetic Literature and in Chronicles.* SBLMS 23 (Missoula: Scholars, 1977).

1 Chronicles 1–9: The Genealogies

We have already noted that the genealogies in the first nine chapters introduce the book of Chronicles and establish continuity with Israel's past.
Thus, 1 Chronicles 1 begins with Adam and goes to Israel (Jacob), branching
out to list the sons of Abraham and the line of Esau. Chapter 9 begins with
the postexilic residents of Jerusalem, connecting with the Chronicler's setting, and then ends with the genealogy of Saul (9:35-44), which leads nicely
into the narrative about his death in ch. 10. In between are the genealogies
for the tribes of Israel, which exhibit the theme of "all Israel." The tribal genealogies are in the following order: Judah (2:3-4:23), Simeon (4:24-43), the
trans-Jordan tribes — Reuben, Gad, half Manasseh (5:1-26) — Levi (6:1-81),
the northern tribes — Issachar (7:1-5), Benjamin (7:6-12), Naphtali (7:13),
Manasseh (7:14-19), Ephraim (7:20-29), Asher (7:30-40), Benjamin (8:1-40).
No genealogies for Dan or Zebulun are included, but this is likely due to ac-
cident in transmission or the like rather than any deliberate exclusion. Both
are listed among the sons of Jacob in 2:1-2 and are therefore part of "all Israel." The two genealogies for Benjamin will be discussed below.

The genealogies in these chapters are frequently lifted from elsewhere in the Hebrew Bible, especially Genesis and Numbers. That this is a
compilation of shorter, independent genealogies is clear from the mixture
of forms of both descending and ascending types. The former trace lines of
descent *from* an ancestor; the latter trace a line from the descendants back
to the ancestor. Examples of descending genealogies are: X begat Y, who
begat Z, etc. and the sons of X (were): Y, his son, Z, his son, etc. An ascending genealogy might run: Z, son of Y, son of X, etc.

Genealogies are often badly misunderstood. They are not static, un-
changing lists but living documents that can be altered to serve social and
political agendas, as well as theological ones.[7] The order in which sons are
listed, for instance, would reflect the relative importance that a genealogist
attaches to the clans that bear their names. Genealogies for the same tribe
or clan can be different at different periods, reflecting changing social and
historical realities. We are especially interested in how the Chronicler has
put together his genealogical lists. The prominence he attaches to Judah
and Levi is reflected in the length and central place in the list of their gene-

7. Robert R. Wilson, *Genealogy and History in the Biblical World.* Yale Near Eastern
Researches 7 (New Haven: Yale University Press, 1977).

alogies. An interesting, more detailed example is the infusion of Samuel, who is elsewhere described as an Ephraimite (1 Sam 1:1), into the Levitical genealogy (1 Chr 6:33), presumably to legitimate his priestly activities.

1 Chronicles 10–2 Chronicles 9: The Reigns of David and Solomon

As indicated, the second major division of Chronicles falls into three sections: the reign of David (1 Chronicles 10–21), the transition from David's reign to Solomon's (1 Chronicles 22–29), and the reign of Solomon (2 Chronicles 1–9).

The Reign of David (1 Chronicles 10–21)

As noted, the account in these chapters is basically borrowed from 2 Samuel, albeit with significant rearrangements and omissions. The section may be outlined in relation to its Samuel source as follows:

1 Chronicles 10//1 Samuel 31	Saul's death
1 Chr 11:1-3//2 Sam 5:1-3	David anointed king of Israel
1 Chr 11:4-9//2 Sam 5:6-10	Conquest of Jerusalem
1 Chr 11:10-47//2 Sam 23:8-39	David's mighty men
1 Chronicles 12// —	Rallying to David
1 Chronicles 13//2 Sam 6:1-11	First attempt to bring up the ark
1 Chronicles 14//2 Sam 5:11-25	Treaty with Hiram of Tyre, defeat of Philistines
1 Chronicles 15–16 [15:25–16:3//2 Sam 6:12-19]	Ark successfully installed in Jerusalem
1 Chronicles 17//2 Samuel 7	Yahweh promises David a dynasty
1 Chronicles 18//2 Samuel 8	David's wars
1 Chronicles 19//2 Samuel 10	Wars with Ammonites and Aramaeans
1 Chr 20:1-3//2 Sam 11:1; 12:26-31	Siege of Rabbah
1 Chr 20:4-8//2 Sam. 21:18-22	Victories over Philistine heroes
1 Chronicles 21//2 Samuel 24	David's census

Careful comparison of Chronicles and Samuel in this section brings the Chronicler's message and interests into clear relief. Chronicles' narrative begins with Saul's death but without any of the stories about his reign found in Samuel. The Chronicler interprets Saul's death and makes clear his reason for beginning at this point in the two verses that he appends to the Samuel version (1 Chr 10:13-14). He ignores the stories about Saul's rejection in 1 Samuel 13 and 15, instead explaining his death and loss of the kingdom on "unfaithfulness," one of his key terms. To illustrate Saul's unfaithfulness, the Chronicler chooses the story of his consultation of the medium of Endor (1 Samuel 28) as a case of failing to "seek" (another key term) Yahweh and instead seeking guidance from an illegitimate source. The kingdom, therefore, was given to David, with whom Chronicles begins its narrative. Some scholars have read Saul's situation as a metaphor for Israel's exile and seeking Yahweh as the Chronicler's prescription for restoration of the nation's greatness under a new Davidic king.

Chronicles' report of David's anointing (1 Chr 11:1-3) closely parallels its Samuel source, except that by omitting the material about the civil war between the houses of Saul and David in 2 Samuel 2–4 the Chronicler leaves no hint that David reigned first over Judah and only later over the united kingdom. In Chronicles, it is "all Israel" united that anoints David as its king from the beginning. To an abbreviated version of the conquest of Jerusalem from Samuel the Chronicler adds the list of David's mighty men, shifting it from its place at the end of 2 Samuel. He also brings in similar lists from elsewhere in order to paint a picture of all Israel joining together to anoint David and conquer Jerusalem (1 Chronicles 11–12).

This same united people then turns its attention to bringing the ark to Jerusalem. The Chronicler, thus, shifts material from Samuel so that David's first thought after conquering the city is to bring up the ark. Only after the first attempt fails (1 Chronicles 13) does David deal with other, more secular matters (1 Chronicles 14). The second, successful attempt to move the ark is the occasion for enormous cultic celebration in Chronicles. Only a small portion of the Chronicles account here is paralleled in Samuel, with most of it being occupied by lists of Levites (1 Chr 15:1-24; 16:4-6, 37-43) and a celebratory psalm (16:7-36) pieced together from parts of Pss 96, 105, and 106.

The Chronicles version of the Davidic promise is very similar to that of its predecessor (2 Samuel 7), though with some minor and meaningful differences. For instance, Chronicles lacks the reference to the possibility that David's son and heir may sin and require discipline (2 Sam 7:14), and it refers to the dynasty ("house") and kingdom not as David's ("your") but as Yahweh's ("my," 1 Chr 17:14). In the next three chapters, the Chronicler borrowed material about David's wars from Samuel in order to emphasize the point of Nathan's oracle that David's function was to prepare for the temple building, not to build it, and to illustrate how David as a "man of blood" was unsuited to build the temple, as explained in the next section (1 Chronicles 22 29). In the case of ch. 20, the Chronicler has united the two parts of the account of the siege of Rabbah in Samuel and omitted the Bathsheba story, which they frame, thus preserving his idealized portrait of David. He sacrifices this portrait somewhat in ch. 21 with the story of David's sinful census. However, as in 10:13-14, the addition in 21:18–22:1 makes clear the reason for its inclusion, as these verses have David specify the location of the future temple's altar on the spot where he sacrifices to end the plague.

The Transition from David's Reign to Solomon's (1 Chronicles 22–29)

The final eight chapters of 1 Chronicles describe David's preparations for the building of the temple and his organization of its personnel. This section is structured as follows.

1 Chronicles 22	David gathers materials and charges Solomon to build the temple
1 Chronicles 23	David organizes the Levites for temple service
1 Chronicles 24	David organizes the priests for temple service
1 Chronicles 25	David organizes the temple musicians
1 Chronicles 26	David organizes the gatekeepers, treasurers, officers, and judges
1 Chronicles 27	David organizes military and civic officials
1 Chronicles 28–29	David instructs Solomon and transfers the kingdom to him

As this outline indicates, the section essentially consists of two large rhetorical units enclosing several sets of lists. Basically, David is portrayed as preparing everything in minute detail — from the blueprint of the temple, which he received from God (28:11-12, 19), to the building materials and workers (22:2-4, 15-16), vessels (28:14-18), and of course orders of person-

127

nel. The temple is to be a magnificent structure, as is appropriate to Yahweh's magnificence (22:5).

In the bracketing speeches, David explains that he wanted to build the temple himself but was prohibited from doing so because he had shed too much blood (28:3). Here, the Chronicler interprets the promise to David in 2 Samuel 7 (//1 Chronicles 17). Forbidding David as a "man of blood" from building the temple probably does not reflect a moral judgment but is rather ritual in nature. That is, David did nothing wrong by shedding blood; indeed, bloodshed was required for him to fulfill his task of bringing the peace necessary for the temple to be built. Solomon, by contrast, was a man of peace (22:9). This is a play on his name: Solomon = shĕlômōh in Hebrew, and "peace" = shālôm. But the idea goes beyond wordplay. Here the Chronicler interprets the theme of "rest" in the Deuteronomistic History (DtrH), where Yahweh promised to establish the centralized "place" (i.e., shrine) for his name to dwell after he had given Israel "rest" from its enemies (cf. Deuteronomy 12). Solomon's reign is a time of peace and rest (both words occur in Hebrew in 1 Chr 22:9) and therefore the appropriate time for the building of the temple. This is the first of three devices that the Chronicler uses to signal Solomon's divine designation as temple builder.

A second such device is the Chronicler's reuse and reinterpretation of the commissioning formula in the DtrH. That formula is found in 22:13, where David tells Solomon, "Be strong and of good courage. Do not be afraid or dismayed." The same formula is found in Moses' commissioning of Joshua (Josh 1:7, 9). Also in 1 Chr 22:13, Solomon is charged to keep the law and its commandments. His success depends on his obedience to them. The difference is that Solomon is not just being commissioned to lead the people as was Joshua. His commission focuses on the building of the temple, and that is how his success will be measured. Thus, in 28:20, the language of commission and God's presence with Solomon are explicitly linked with the task of completing the work on the temple.

A third device is found in the use of the verb "to choose" in David's closing speeches in chs. 28–29. Just as Yahweh chose the tribe of Judah and from it David to be ruler, so he has chosen Solomon from among David's sons (28:4-5), and Solomon has been chosen specifically for the purpose of building the temple (28:6; 29:1).

The relatively simple structure of this section masks the literary complexities and signs of creativity that it contains. In ch. 24, for instance, many scholars believe the list of priests in vv. 1-19 to be an insertion because it interrupts the listing of Levites, which seems to continue from ch. 23 in 24:20-31. Also, one would expect the priests to be given primacy in the set of lists before the Levites. These kinds of observations have led some scholars to posit the hand of one or more later editors in these lists. The motive for such additions, as for the Chronicler's original lists, was the powerful legitimation they provided for groups and vocations at the writers' time period. Thus, chs. 22–29 as a whole make the claim that the divisions and duties listed in them go back to David and were established by his and/or divine authority. In some cases, moreover, the lists claim Levitical descent for certain offices, such as that of the gatekeepers (26:1-19).

The Reign of Solomon (2 Chronicles 1–9)

As might be expected, the account of Solomon's reign is focused on the temple: his preparations for its construction (ch. 2), the construction proper (3:1–5:1), and its dedication (5:2–7:22). The framework in 1:1-17 + 8:1–9:31 describes Solomon's wealth, wisdom, and international prestige, but even these traits help to serve the temple project. Solomon's wealth furnishes the materials for building; his wisdom motivates him to complete the project; and his international ties provide the skilled labor for its design and construction. Another structural device in these chapters is the series of notices about stages in the temple construction. The notice in 2:1 announces Solomon's intention to build and 3:1 the start of construction. Then, 5:1; 7:1; and 8:1 note the completion of the temple construction, its dedication, and all of Solomon's projects, respectively.

As in 1 Chronicles, the Chronicler borrows heavily from the DtrH for his account of Solomon. Most of 1 Chronicles 1–9 is loosely parallel to 1 Kings 1–10. However, as the word "loosely" implies, the Chronicler did not follow his source as closely when he drew from it for Solomon as he did for David. The Chronicler's method here might best be characterized as abridgement and adaptation. The changes can be subtle but meaningful. A case in point is 2 Chr 1:8-9, where Solomon asks Yahweh to fulfill his promise to David in an abbreviated revision of 1 Kgs 3:6-8. This alludes to the Davidic promise in 1 Chronicles 17, but since Solomon has already succeeded David, it must refer more specifically to the statement in 17:12 that David's son would build the temple. The Chronicler also alluded to other texts, perhaps portraying the temple as the climax of Israel's religious traditions, as when he refers to the people being more numerous than the dust of the earth (1:9), drawing on the patriarchal promise in Genesis.

One might expect Chronicles' version of the temple construction to be longer and more detailed, but such is not the case. It is also abridged as compared with 1 Kings 6–7. The Chronicler was apparently less concerned with details of architecture and furnishing and more interested in showing the temple's lavishness. Again he draws not only on Kings for the description of items used in the worship but also on that of the tabernacle in Exodus and on the temple of his own day. In this way, he stresses the continuity of Israel's cultic traditions.

Solomon's transfer of the ark into the temple in ch. 5 corresponds to David's transfer of the ark to Jerusalem. As in the former story, Solomon gathers all Israel for the occasion and offers great numbers of sacrifices. At the end of the chapter, the descent of Yahweh's cloud and glory upon the temple recalls the inauguration of the tabernacle (Exod 40:34-35). Similarly, the fire from heaven that devours the sacrifices upon the altar at the dedication of the temple (2 Chr 7:1-3) evokes the inauguration of the tabernacle and of Aaron's priesthood (Lev 9:23-24) as well as the story of David's designation of the site in 1 Chronicles 21.

Chronicles' account of Solomon ends with the visit of the queen of Sheba, which then leads into a summary of his wealth. Her speech in praise of Solomon (2 Chr 9:5-8) is a fitting theological synthesis of the Chronicler's presentation of his reign. Solomon's wealth and wisdom are tangible signs of Yahweh's love for Israel. They are rewards for Solomon's faithfulness as well as the means through which he faithfully fulfills the charge to build the temple. His role as temple builder balances David's as the one who founds the dynasty and creates the conditions allowing the temple to be built. This is quite a different ending from the one in 1 Kings 11, which narrates Solomon's apostasy. The Chronicler evidently had no choice but to omit that story, given the significance he attached to the temple and his doctrine of reward/retribution.

2 Chronicles 10–36: The Kingdom of Judah

The order of kings in Chronicles is the same as that found in 1-2 Kings, which again served as the Chronicler's principal source. However, there are significant differences between the two works in both overall presentation and the details regarding individual kings. Two general differences that have already been mentioned are the omission in Chronicles of materials dealing with the northern kingdom, except where these overlap with Judah, and the tendency of Chronicles to "periodize" kings' reigns by having a portion characterized by faithfulness and reward be followed by a portion of disobedience and punishment, or the other way around. In cases of individual kings, Chronicles' narrative sometimes varies extensively from Kings as the Chronicler seeks his own agenda and objectives. While it is impossible here to treat each reign at length, we can sketch the basic contours of the Chronicler's presentation of each king as it compares with Kings and as it fits Chronicles' overall plan and message.

Rehoboam (2 Chronicles 10–12)

Chronicles' presentation of Rehoboam falls into three distinct segments corresponding to the chapter divisions and is highly ambivalent. The first chapter (2 Chronicles 10) narrates the division of Israel (the northern kingdom) from Judah. The Chronicler could not accept the explanation of Kings that this was the result of Solomon's apostasy. In Chronicles, it was caused by Jeroboam's rebelliousness combined with Rehoboam's pride and naiveté. The former point will be elaborated on later in Chronicles. Rehoboam's arrogance and foolishness are apparent in the story. The statement in v. 15 that the division was brought about by God is borrowed from 1 Kgs 12:15 and causes a theological problem in Chronicles, since the Chronicler does not view it as divine judgment on Solomon. Perhaps the initial division was to be understood as judgment for Rehoboam's pride and the continued state of division as rebellion.

In ch. 11, the orientation toward Rehoboam is essentially positive. His military fortifications (vv. 5-12), strengthening by the priests and Levites who come to Jerusalem from the north (vv. 13-17), and large prosperous family (vv. 18-23) are all signs of divine blessing in Chronicles. They apparently accrue to Rehoboam because he listens to the prophet Shemaiah and does not go to war against Israel (11:1-4//1 Kgs 12:21-24). However, this positive period in his reign is counterbalanced by a negative period detailed in the next chapter whereby the Chronicler accounts for Shishak's invasion as brought on by Rehoboam's pride and disobedience

(12:1-12, based on 1 Kgs 14:25-31). Even so, Rehoboam humbled himself and avoided total destruction (12:7, 12). An item of special note in the Rehoboam account is the different meanings Chronicles attributes to "Israel" as referring to north and south united (10:1?), the north alone (10:3, 16-17; 11:16), or Judah and Benjamin, along with the "faithful" northerners as "true" Israel (11:3; 12:1, 6).

Abijah (2 Chronicles 13)

Since Rehoboam was unsuitable as a model for future kings of Judah, the Chronicler turned to the next king, Abijah, for that purpose. This meant adjusting the perspective in 1 Kgs 15:1-8, which is negative toward Abijah but also lacks much detail about his reign. The Chronicler therefore, retained only the introduction and conclusion from Kings and infused the account of Abijah's reign with his own unique content (2 Chr 13:3-21). The Chronicler used the references in Kings to war between Abijah and Jeroboam as the setting for his account, which consists largely of a speech by Abijah to Jeroboam and his army (vv. 4-12). The speech is important for its clear expression of the Chronicler's view of the north. That view, as we have seen, is that since Yahweh gave the kingship of Israel to David and his descendants, Jeroboam and the northerners have rebelled against Yahweh. They have exacerbated their sin by worshipping other gods and adopting variant cultic practices and personnel. They remain part of Yahweh's chosen people, but they need to repent and return to the legitimate political and religious institutions of Judah. Abijah's model behavior is apparent not only in his speech but also in his deportment and that of his people in the battle that follows. When they are ambushed by Jeroboam's forces, they cry out to Yahweh. Their trust is rewarded when Yahweh defeats the Israelites.

Asa (2 Chronicles 14–16)

Chronicles' account of Asa's reign is significantly longer than Kings' and again largely the Chronicler's composition. Its main message is succinctly expressed in 2 Chr 15:2: "Yahweh is with you while you are with him. If you seek him, he will be found by you, but if you abandon him, he will abandon you." The Chronicler illustrates this message by means of two threats to Asa and his contrasting responses. The account begins by noting that for the first ten years of Asa's reign the land had rest (14:1), a reward and blessing not enjoyed since Solomon. Asa's religious reforms bring further rewards in the form of building projects, a large army, and peace and prosperity (14:3-8). His response to the threat of Zerah the Ethiopian is to cry out for help to Yahweh, who delivers him (14:9-15). This leads to the prophetic oracle of assurance (15:1-7), which in turn calls forth further reforms and a rededication to Yahweh (15:8-19).

In the last five years of Asa's reign (ch. 16) things take a turn for the worse. The Chronicler adopts this move in part as a theological explanation of the notice in 1 Kgs 15:23 about Asa's disease at the end of his life. He finds this explanation in Asa's alliance with a foreign king (1 Kgs 15:18-20), which he interprets as a failure to "cry out" to Yahweh. He elaborates the Kings account with the oracle of Hanani and Asa's reaction to it (16:7-10), thus providing an antithesis to Asa's handling of the threat from Zerah in order to illustrate the importance of relying on God.

Jehoshaphat (2 Chronicles 17–20)

The length of Chronicles' account of Jehoshaphat's reign indicates his significance and the Chronicler's positive orientation toward him. At the same time, Chronicles does evince some ambiguity toward this king because of his alliance with the northern kingdom, which has long-lasting consequences. The opening description of Jehoshaphat's reign (2 Chr 17:1-6) is very positive both in terms of his devotion to Yahweh and the rewards he receives. His mission to teach the law (17:7-9) leads to even greater rewards in terms of international prestige, building projects, and military prowess (17:10-19).

Nevertheless, Jehoshaphat's alliance with Ahab of Israel (ch. 18) sullies his reputation. This is the only extended narrative about the north in Kings that is duplicated in Chronicles, and it is the source of the Chronicler's ambivalence about Jehoshaphat. The Chronicler's changes are few and minor. He enhances Jehoshaphat's wealth (18:1-20) and presents him as the superior, whom Ahab exploits for selfish purposes. He also has the prophet Micaiah use plural verbs, thereby addressing both kings and not just Ahab as in Kings. The greatest change, though, comes in v. 31, where Jehoshaphat cries out, not in panic as in Kings, but to Yahweh, who then helps him. Despite his alliance with the wicked king, then, and his failure to regard the warning of Yahweh's prophet, whose advice he required, Jehoshaphat retains his trust in Yahweh. The ambivalence continues in 19:2-3, unique in Chronicles, where Jehoshaphat is condemned and threatened by a prophet because of his alliance, but then the threat seems to be mitigated or withdrawn. In contrast to his father Asa, Jehoshaphat also does not lash out at the prophet. Indeed, the rest of this chapter sees him going out personally among the people, restoring them to Yahweh and appointing judges who will adjudicate matters among them according to the law. This episode reflects an extended pun on Jehoshaphat's name, which means "Yahweh judges."

The last chapter about Jehoshaphat (20) is unique to Chronicles. It consists of another battle account that contrasts markedly with the one in ch. 18. Here, Jehoshaphat defends his country rather than aiding an ally in an offensive strike. His model response is to seek help from God (vv. 3-4) by calling on his people to join him in crying out to Yahweh (vv. 5-12). This evokes a reassuring divine response mediated through a Levitical singer (vv. 13-17) followed by Yahweh's defeat of the enemy and quiet and rest for the remainder of Jehoshaphat's reign (vv. 22-30).

The conclusion to Jehoshaphat's reign is borrowed from 1 Kgs 22:41-49 with several interesting changes. In describing Jehoshaphat's failure to remove the high places (v. 33), Chronicles stresses the interior, spiritual nature of the sin rather than the ritual issues. He refers to a prophetic source ("the Annals of Jehu son of Hanani") imbedded within the "Book of the Kings of Israel." The former is likely fictional and the latter a reference to the book of Kings. The notice about Jehoshaphat's ship-building venture (vv. 35-37) interprets the shipwreck in 1 Kgs 22:48 as a joint venture, ignoring Jehoshaphat's refusal to engage in such a venture in the next verse. Since 2 Chr 9:21 (//1 Kgs 10:22) notes Solomon's success at shipping, the Chronicler here may be making the point that Jehoshaphat, for all of his virtues and success, did not live up to the model set by Solomon.

Jehoram (2 Chronicles 21)

The ambivalence about Jehoshaphat continues through the next three chapters as Chronicles narrates the negative results of his alliance with Ahab in the three rulers who succeeded him. Jehoram's murderous treatment of his brothers (2 Chr 21:4) is reminiscent of the typical dynastic transition in the north as described in Kings. Jehoram follows in the way of Ahab and the kings of the north because of his marriage to Ahab's daughter (v. 6). Yet the Chronicler stresses the endurance of the dynasty because of God's promise to David, and this is his theme for Jehoram and the two monarchs who follow him. The successful revolts of Edom and Libnah (cf. 2 Kgs 8:20-22) are seen as punishment for Jehoram's sins. As is often the case in Chronicles, a prophetic warning — here in the form of a letter from Elijah — precedes further punishment (21:12-15). The rest of the account sees the fulfillment of Elijah's threats. The survival of Jehoram's youngest son, Jehoahaz (called Ahaziah in ch. 22), saves the dynasty from extinction in implicit accord with the Davidic promise. A series of statements about the absence of formalities and regret in the wake of Jehoram's agonizing death reflect the Chronicler's contemptuous attitude toward him (vv. 18-20).

Ahaziah (2 Chr 22:1-9)

Ahaziah is also a casualty of Jehoshaphat's alliance with the Omride dynasty of Israel (2 Chr 22:2-4). His renewal of that alliance through a joint military expedition leads to his downfall at the hands of the rebel Israelite general Jehu (vv. 5-9). Here the Chronicler abridges and adapts the story in 2 Kings 8–10, making Ahaziah's death the focus as ordained by God (2 Chr 22:7). He is only granted burial because of his kinship with Jehoshaphat (v. 9).

<Athaliah (2 Chr 22:10–23:21)>

The power vacuum that results from Ahaziah's death is filled by Athaliah, Ahab's daughter, who threatens to invalidate the Davidic promise by wiping out the royal line (2 Chr 22:10). Hence, the brackets in the heading above. The focus of the narrative is on the preservation of the legitimate heir and Athaliah's overthrow. There are no other details about her seven-year rule, and even the usual regnal formulas are lacking because she is regarded as illegitimate. The legitimate heir, Joash, is saved by another woman of royal descent, Jehoshabeath, whose name resembles Jehoshaphat's and who is married to the priest Jehoiada. The overthrow is led by priests and Levites who bring representatives of all Israel into a covenant

(23:3) to proclaim Joash king. Under Jehoiada, cultic reforms are initiated and the temple is cleansed and properly restored to the care of the Levites (vv. 16-19). The story as a whole illustrates the durability of the Davidic dynasty under divine promise and contrasts it with the apostate kings of Israel. It also highlights the importance of the priests and Levites for guiding the nation in the right direction.

Joash (2 Chronicles 24)

The Joash of Kings (2 Kings 12) is a religious reformer who nonetheless suffers invasion and assassination. Such a portrait would never do for the Chronicler, who therefore periodizes Joash's reign. Joash is righteous and carries out extensive repairs on the temple so long as his priestly mentor, Jehoiada, is alive (2 Chr 24:1-14). After the death of Jehoiada, who is treated much like a king in Chronicles (vv. 15-16), Joash heeds bad advice and strays into idolatry (vv. 17-18). Following the typical pattern in Chronicles, there are warnings by prophets, one of whom is Jehoiada's son (vv. 19-20). Joash ignores the warnings and kills his mentor's son (vv. 21-22). Joash's defeat and assassination then follow as divine punishments for his misdoings (vv. 23-27).

Amaziah (2 Chronicles 25)

This king's reign also consists of two distinct periods — good and evil, hence the Chronicler's judgment that he did right, albeit not with a pure heart (2 Chr 25:2). In the first part of his reign, Amaziah heeds a prophetic warning against incorporating Israelites into his army and instead to rely upon God. As a result, he is victorious against the Edomites (vv. 5-13). This anecdote is a theological elaboration of 2 Kgs 14:7 and the greatest difference between the Chronicles and Kings versions on Amaziah. However, he then commits idolatry with the Edomite gods and ignores and even threatens a prophet sent to admonish him (2 Chr 25:14-16). True to the prophet's word, therefore, his punishment comes in the form of defeat and the ransacking of Jerusalem when he provokes Joash of Israel to war (vv. 17-24). As for other kings, the Chronicler's handling of his source material in Kings implies that disaster did not occur arbitrarily or without adequate prophetic warning.

Uzziah (2 Chronicles 26)

The brief account of Uzziah (= Azariah) in 2 Kgs 15:1-7 contains two details that to the Chronicler's mind stood in tension — his exceptionally long (fifty-two years) reign and his leprosy. The Chronicler explained that Uzziah had done right in the same way as his father Amaziah, i.e., for only the first part of his reign, as long as the prophet Zechariah was alive (2 Chr 26:4-5). During that period "God made him prosper" through military victory, international prestige, building projects, and a powerful army (vv. 6-15), not to mention his long reign. But his strength fostered arrogance, which led him to attempt to usurp priestly duties, and for that reason God struck him with leprosy (vv. 16-21).

Jotham (2 Chronicles 27)

In contrast to his recent predecessors, Jotham remains righteous through-out his reign. The Chronicler thus elaborates only briefly in comparison with Kings on Jotham's rewards, which included building projects and military victories followed by tribute (2 Chr 27:3-5). In sum, "Jotham became strong because he ordered his ways before Yahweh" (v. 6). As a further indication of his righteousness, in Chronicles he is the first king since Jehoshaphat to be honored with burial in the royal tombs (v. 9).

Ahaz (2 Chronicles 28)

The Chronicler reworked the account of Ahaz in 2 Kings 16 in order to present him as the worst king of Judah. His statement in 2 Chr 28:19 best sums up his presentation: Yahweh brought Judah low because of Ahaz's unrestrained evil behavior and faithlessness. Thus, after detailing Ahaz's wicked deeds (vv. 1-4), he launches into a litany of the defeats suffered by Judah under Ahaz at the hands of Aram, Israel, Assyria, and the Philistines (vv. 5-21). Instead of learning from the defeats and repenting, Ahaz acted even more faithlessly by adopting the gods of Damascus (vv. 22-23), not just duplicating an altar from Damascus as in Kings. His apostasy reached epic proportions when he closed the doors of the temple in Jerusalem (v. 24). It is difficult to imagine a more damning indictment from the

Chronicler. Perhaps the most interesting feature of this account is the story of the capture and return of the people of Judah by Israelites, which is unique to 2 Chr 28:8-15. Despite the comparison of Ahaz's depravity to that of the kings of Israel (v. 2), the obedience of these Israelites to the prophetic word emphasizes the kinship of Israel and Judah as God's people and shows that there are yet people in the north who are attentive to the divine word. The account as a whole paves the way nicely for the reunification of the kingdoms under Ahaz's successor.

Hezekiah (2 Chronicles 29–32)

The length of the account of Hezekiah's reign suggests the Chronicler's positive perspective on him, especially since only 2 Chronicles 32 shows close affinity to the Kings account. The evaluation that he did right just as David had done (2 Chr 29:2) is used for only one other king in Chronicles, namely Josiah. Hezekiah's righteous acts begin in the very first month of his reign when he reopens the temple and summons the Levites to cleanse it and restore the cult (29:3-11). As worship is restored, Hezekiah also stations the Levitical musicians in their proper places according to the order established by David (29:25-30). Thus, in much the same way as David and Solomon are model kings for their joint role in building the temple and setting up its cult, Hezekiah is a paradigm of a king who restores the temple and its worship. His people also model the proper attitude of willing hearts in providing sacrifices (29:31-36).

The account of Hezekiah's Passover in ch. 30 illustrates not only his devotion to proper worship and ritual but also his interest in the people of the north, who are invited to return to Yahweh and the temple (30:8). Hezekiah prays on behalf of those who do come but are not ritually clean (vv. 18-19). This, plus his change of the date for keeping the festival (vv. 2-3) seem to reflect the idea that the right attitude trumps exact ritual observance because God is merciful. The whole scene is portrayed as one of great joy, and it is prolonged for a second week, as was the original celebration of the dedication of the temple under Solomon. The notice that no such celebration had been seen in Jerusalem since David and Solomon (v. 26) again shows the Chronicler's high esteem for Hezekiah. The celebration has lasting benefits, as the people remove paraphernalia associated with the worship of other gods throughout Judah and even in northern territories (31:1), such that Hezekiah is portrayed as reuniting Israel and Judah to some extent. His further organization of the priests and Levites in this chapter again likens him to David.

In the face of Sennacherib's threat Hezekiah's behavior is again exemplary as he encourages his commanders on the grounds that God is with them and will fight for them (32:7-8). Yahweh does deliver Hezekiah, and the resulting rest (v. 22) is yet another point of likeness between his era and that of David and Solomon. Even the obscure note that Hezekiah failed to respond appropriately to God's sign in his illness is followed by the reference to his humbling himself (vv. 24-26).

Manasseh (2 Chr 33:1-20)

Kings attributes both the longest (fifty-five years) and the worst reign to Manasseh. This is a theological impossibility for the Chronicler, for whom longevity is a reward for righteousness. He resolves the tension by periodizing, uniquely portraying the first part of Manasseh's reign as evil and the second as good. The transition occurs when Manasseh is in exile in Babylon, in anticipation of what will soon happen to Judah. He repents in Babylon and is restored to his throne, where he is blessed with building projects and a formidable army. Manasseh thus illustrates the power and effectiveness of repentance.

Amon (2 Chr 33:21-25)

Chronicles' account of Amon matches the Kings version in brevity and for the most part in content. Amon follows the early ways of his father, Manasseh, whose repentance is effective only for himself.

Josiah (2 Chronicles 34–35)

In Kings, Josiah's reforms make him the greatest king of Judah; in Chronicles, Josiah takes a back seat to Hezekiah as a reforming king. The Chronicler focuses his account on Josiah's Passover celebration and significantly expands the Kings version. The Kings account has Josiah begin his reforms in his tenth year as king when he was eighteen years old. The Chronicler could not abide the idea that he had tolerated the perversions in Jerusalem for so long. Hence, he described the reforms beginning already in Josiah's eighth year, with the book of the law being discovered in the eighteenth year. Thus, the lawbook was not the impulse for reform as in Kings but a reward for Josiah's personal piety, which spurred the reforms. Also, since Manasseh had already corrected his own apostasies in the temple, Josiah's reforms were concentrated on the rest of Jerusalem and areas of the north (2 Chr 34:3, 5-6). As one might expect, the Chronicler gives significant place to the Levites in Josiah's reforms and especially in his account of the Passover, with appeals to the authority of David and Solomon as well as Moses and Aaron. Finally, the Kings version of Josiah's death at Pharaoh Neco's hand following all of his reforms posed a theological problem for the Chronicler. He adjusted the account such that Josiah's refusal to heed the divine warning mediated through Neco himself was what brought about his demise.

Jehoahaz (2 Chr 36:1-4), Jehoiakim (36:5-7), Jehoiachin (36:8-10), and Zedekiah (36:11-14)

The last four kings of Judah are all dealt with in summary fashion in Chronicles. Most of this material (2 Chr 36:1-12a) is an abridgement of 2 Kgs 23:31–25:30. To this the Chronicler added his account of the fall of Jerusalem and the exile (2 Chr 36:12b-21). Then, Cyrus's edict (vv. 22-23) was appended either by the Chronicler or at a later stage. The result is that the book now ends on a positive note. Among the final four kings, the account of Zedekiah is especially interesting. In accord with his doctrine of individual responsibility, the Chronicler blames the exile on Zedekiah and the people of his generation who acted unfaithfully (v. 14). The same word, "unfaithful," is used of Saul in 1 Chr 10:13, thus providing a bracket around the book's narrative. But the fact that Zedekiah's fate is not told in Chronicles as it is in Kings leaves the reader with a sense of openness about the Davidic dynasty. Add to this the fact that the Chronicler speaks of the exile as a Sabbath (2 Chr 36:21) and that Yahweh's compassion toward his people is evident in that the exile was a last resort after God had persistently warned them (v. 15). All of these ingredients in Chronicles open the way toward future restoration or resumption of the kingdom.

The foregoing survey makes it clear that the Chronicler basically rewrites the history of the kings of Judah in the book of Kings, interpreting it through his own theological principles. His frequent periodization of the reigns of individual kings is not an end in itself but simply a tool by which he effects his theological interpretation. To put it in other words, the history of Judah is not so much the objective of the Chronicler's narrative as the setting or forum for the presentation of his theology.

9

Ezra-Nehemiah

The final example of the Bible's Historical Literature to be discussed in this volume is the book of Ezra-Nehemiah. I say "book," because Ezra and Nehemiah are treated as a single book in the Hebrew Bible. However, Christian tradition has regarded them as separate books at least from the time of the third-century Christian scholar Origen. Whether they were originally distinct works is hard to say. Most scholars think they were not. If they did originally exist as separate works it would explain some of the repetitiousness between the two, such as the list of returnees in Ezra 2 that is duplicated in Nehemiah 7. However, Ezra's public reading of the law in fulfillment of his mission, which takes place in Nehemiah 8, attests the unity of Ezra-Nehemiah in its present form.

As discussed in Chapter Two above, Ezra-Nehemiah is probably best regarded as a distinct work from Chronicles. Most scholars today regard it as such, and I will treat it that way here. At the same time, the repetition of the Cyrus edict (2 Chr 36:22-23; Ezra 1:1-4) indicates some kind of link between the two works, such that Ezra-Nehemiah seems to have been intended at some stage of development as the continuation of the story in Chronicles. Chronicles ends with the exile of the people of Judah to Babylon, which it refers to as a seventy-year Sabbath for the land, followed by Cyrus's edict releasing the exiles to return home to Judah to rebuild the temple (2 Chr 36:17-23). Ezra-Nehemiah picks up the story there and recounts how the returnees rebuilt their temple, their community, and their city.

Structure

These three rebuilding efforts focused on temple, community, and city furnish the general structure of Ezra-Nehemiah. It is generally recognized that the book is built around three main accomplishments of restoration: the rebuilding of the temple (Ezra 1–6), the rebuilding of the community (Ezra 7–10), and the rebuilding of the walls of Jerusalem (Nehemiah 1–7). Within this overall framework one finds more sophisticated structural components. For instance, the two essentially identical lists of returnees in Ezra 2 and Nehemiah 7 effectively frame these accomplishments. There is also a similar plot line for each of the three, as each is commissioned by the Persian king and equipped with appropriate documentation in the form of an edict or letter(s). Each section then narrates the difficulties encountered by the leading character in carrying out his mission and his ultimate success.

The remaining chapters of Nehemiah can be connected with individual missions. Ezra's reading of the law and the people's promise to obey it (Nehemiah 8–10), as noted, is the climax of his mission. Hence, Ezra 7–10 + Nehemiah 8–10 might be considered the complete section dealing with the rebuilding of the community. Similarly, the repopulation of Jerusalem and rededication of its walls (Neh 11:1–13:3) followed by the account of Nehemiah's second visit (13:4-31) conclude the account of his mission, so that Nehemiah 1–7 + 11–13 could be construed as the section of the book detailing the rebuilding of Jerusalem. Nonetheless, as the book now stands, Nehemiah 8–13 provide a climax and celebration of all three accomplishments. Put another way, the three acts of rebuilding — the temple, the community, and Jerusalem — are presented as three parts of one package of restoration that builds toward the reading of the law and ceremonies of rededication and celebration in Nehemiah 8–13.

Sources

Much of the narratives of Ezra's and Nehemiah's missions is in the first person and therefore purports, at least implicitly, to be first-hand accounts of the events they describe. Scholars typically refer to two extended first person sources or "memoirs" that they believe served as the basis for these materials. The "Ezra memoir" lay behind Ezra 7–10 + Nehemiah 8–9, and the "Nehemiah memoir" behind Nehemiah 1–7; 11:1-2; 12:31-43; 13:4-31. The

Nehemiah memoir, at least, seems to have been an authentic document, Nehemiah's report of his activities, perhaps for the purpose of courting royal and divine favor (cf. Neh 13:31).

Intermixed with these two primary sources are a number of other materials that purport or appear to be discrete documents. These are of various genres, including royal decrees (Ezra 1:2-4; 6:3-5), letters (Ezra 4:11-22; 5:7-17; 6:6-12; 7:12-26; Neh 6:2-9), inventories of temple vessels (Ezra 1:9-11; 8:26-27), and personnel rosters and rolls (Ezra 2:1-70 = Neh 7:7-72a; Ezra 8:1-14; 10:18-43; Neh 3:1-32; 10:1-27; 11:3-24, 25-36; 12:1-26). To get a sense of the extent of Ezra-Nehemiah that such source documents comprise, it may help to list them in the order in which they appear in the book:

Ezra	1:2-4	Cyrus decree
	1:9-11	inventory of temple vessels
	2:1-70	roster of returnees
	4:11-22	letter of Rehum and Shimshai to Artaxerxes and response
	5:7-17	letter of Tattenai to Darius
	6:3-5	decree of Cyrus concerning the temple
	6:6-12	letter of Darius to Tattenai
	7:12-26	letter of Artaxerxes to Ezra
	8:1-14	heads of families who returned with Ezra
	8:26-27	roster of temple vessels
	10:18-43	roster of men who married foreign women
Neh	3:1-32	roster of builders of city wall of Jerusalem
	6:2-9	exchange between Nehemiah and Sanballat
	7:7-72a	roster of returnees
	10:1-27	signees to Nehemiah's covenant
	11:3-24	roll of residents of Jerusalem
	11:25-36	roll of residents of Judah and Benjamin
	12:1-26	roster of priests

Even this list does not adequately represent the extent to which source documents, whether purported or real, have influenced the composition of Ezra-Nehemiah. In the first place, it does not include other materials possibly derived from sources, such as prayers (Ezra 9:6-15; Neh 1:5-11; 9:6-37). What is more, the list above does not include introductions and conclusions to such sources that may have been composed to accommodate them to the narrative. The documents, or some of them, namely the letters, may have come to the author of Ezra-Nehemiah as a collection. This would help to explain a peculiar feature of the book — the fact that it is written partly in Hebrew and partly in Aramaic. The letters are all found within the Aramaic section of the book (Ezra 4:8–6:18; 7:12-26), suggesting that they were retained as official correspondence between Jerusalem and the Persian authorities. On the other hand, the use of Aramaic for the section of the book containing the letters may well be a literary device designed to give the impression of their authenticity. Indeed, while scholars have generally been inclined to regard these documents as genuine, the possibility that at least some of them are imitations must be borne in mind. This is not just reflective of a healthy caution where the Bible's claims about historical sources are concerned. There is no unambiguous evidence for the existence of contemporary documents exhibiting this kind of interest in local religious matters nor does there appear to have been any imperial policy of religious tolerance. Rather than tolerance, the operative idea was apparently flexibility and variety. That is, the Persians were willing to work within local norms and according to local customs and laws so long as these did not conflict with the empire's larger interests.[1]

History

The mention of the Persians and Persian policy raises the matter of the relationship of Ezra-Nehemiah to history. Ezra-Nehemiah is our most important source for the history of Judah, now the Persian province of Yehud, during the period following the return from Babylonian exile. At the same time, there is a great deal more going on in Ezra-Nehemiah than the straightforward narration of history. It is a sophisticated work of literature and theology. As a result, the historical background and setting of this period raise a number of problems for the book, which we will examine below. A more positive way of looking at this matter is to say that the historical background and setting are crucial for understanding what the author of the book is doing in the arenas of literature and theology.

---

1. See Amélie Kuhrt, *The Persian Empire: A Corpus of Sources from the Achaemenid Period* (London: Routledge, 2007) 1:828-30; and "Persia, Persians," *DOTHB*, 768-82.

The Persian Empire in the Hebrew Bible

The Persian Empire is also known as the Achaemenid Empire after the eponymous founder of its ruling dynasty. Headquartered in modern Iran, the Persian Empire gained ascendancy ca. 550 B.C.E. and became the largest empire the world had ever seen until its conquest by Alexander the Great ca. 330 B.C.E. King Cyrus II "the Great" was the Achaemenid ruler who founded the empire through his military conquests, which included Babylon in 539. The Persians, as suggested, exercised flexibility where matters of local administration were concerned, and apparently on those grounds allowed former residents of Judah and Jerusalem who had been in exile in Babylon to return to their homeland. The biblical writers celebrate Cyrus as an instrument of Yahweh (2 Chr 36:22; Ezra 1:1), Second Isaiah even referring to him as Yahweh's shepherd and anointed one (Isa 44:28; 45:1). Cyrus's edict in Ezra-Nehemiah sets the tone for what is basically a positive orientation toward the Persian Empire, as the Persian kings are consistently portrayed as agents of Yahweh and supporters of the reconstruction efforts.

Beginning with Cyrus, the Persian kings who are relevant for Ezra-Nehemiah and the dates of their reigns are as follows.[2]

Cyrus II (559-530)
Cambyses II (530-522)
Bardiya (522)
Darius I (522-486)
Xerxes (486-465)[3]
Artaxerxes I (465-424/423)
Darius II (423-405)
Artaxerxes II (405-359/358)

Within this chronological framework, Ezra-Nehemiah narrates a rebuilding process in three stages (temple, community, city), as we have seen, but under four different leaders. The four, with the dates most commonly attributed to them, are:

2. Adapted from Kuhrt, "Persia, Persians," 775.
3. Also called Ahasuerus (Ezra 4:6), this king is prominent in the book of Esther.

Sheshbazzar (538)
Zerubbabel (520-515)
Ezra (458)
Nehemiah (445-433)

Difficulties emerge in trying to relate these individual leaders and their activities as detailed in the narrative of Ezra-Nehemiah to one another within the historical framework of the Persian imperial monarchy. These difficulties are more frequently resolved on the literary level — by appeal to the author's objectives and techniques — than by proposed adjustments to fit historical circumstances. Two examples in Ezra 1–6 illustrate.

The first example concerns the correspondence of Rehum and Shimshai with Artaxerxes in Ezra 4:7-24. In its setting in Ezra 4, the correspondence serves to explain the delay in the construction of the temple under Zerubbabel (4:1-5). Zerubbabel and his collaborators succeeded in rebuilding the temple in 515, fifty years before Artaxerxes I came to the throne in 465. The content of the correspondence, moreover, concerns not the building of the temple but the building of the walls of Jerusalem, which was accomplished substantially later than the building of the temple. Clearly, then, the account of the correspondence is out of chronological order. This is probably best explained as the author's use of such correspondence, albeit from a later period, to illustrate the kind of opposition faced by the returnees on the part of the "people of the land," i.e., the locals who had not gone into exile. In this same vein, v. 6 refers to another letter, not duplicated here, from these same "people of the land" to King Ahasuerus (Xerxes), who reigned 486-465, before Artaxerxes but still well after the temple had been completed in 515.

The second example also relates to the gap between the completion of the temple in 515 and events in Artaxerxes's reign more than fifty years later. In fact, it is precisely this gap that lies between chs. 6 and 7 of Ezra. Chapter 6 ends with an account of the celebration of the Passover at the newly reconstructed temple in Jerusalem. Chapter 7 then begins by relating Ezra's journey from Babylon to Jerusalem in the seventh year of Artaxerxes's reign or 458, nearly sixty years after the completion of the temple described at the end of Ezra 6. The reason for this gap may be due in part to a lack of sources for these years available to the author, but it also indicates the author's interest in recounting what he perceived as stages of return and rebuilding under distinct leaders. Other difficulties concerning the relationship of these leaders to one another have been matters of considerable debate among scholars and will now be discussed separately.

Sheshbazzar and Zerubbabel

In Ezra 1, the individual whom King Cyrus commissions to lead the returnees in rebuilding the temple is Sheshbazzar (1:5-10). As this was the year following Cyrus's conquest of Babylon, called his "first year" in Ezra 1:1, it was 538 B.C.E. In Ezra 5:14-16, Sheshbazzar is called governor and credited with having laid the foundation of the temple, but other than that, he disappears from Ezra-Nehemiah without explanation. In fact, he is not mentioned anywhere else in the Bible, so nothing more is known of him. The title "prince of Judah" (Ezra 1:8) suggests his Davidic ancestry, but there is no genealogy given for him. This may be due to ideological factors in Ezra-Nehemiah, i.e., the book's acceptance of Persian rule and the apparent absence of any hope in the restoration of the Davidic monarchy. Sheshbazzar has been identified with Shenazzar, a member of the Davidic house and the uncle of Zerubbabel according to 1 Chr 3:18, but this identification is contested.

More is known about Zerubbabel. He is called the son of Pedaiah in 1 Chr 3:19, but elsewhere Shealtiel is named as his father (Ezra 3:2, 8; 5:2; Neh 12:1; Hag 1:1, 12, 14; 2:2, 23). Whatever the reason for this difference, Zerubbabel is presented throughout the books of Haggai and Zechariah as the governor of Judah and the heir to David's throne. In Ezra-Nehemiah, he is the leader of a wave of returnees from Babylon (Ezra 2:2; Neh 12:1) who succeed in rebuilding the temple (Ezra 3:2 [= Neh 7:7], 8). However, the missions of Sheshbazzar and Zerubbabel are not clearly distinguished, so that it is uncertain whether or when they overlapped. Nor is it clear when Zerubbabel arrived in Jerusalem. Ezra 4 seems to place him there already in the reign of Cyrus, though local opposition prevents him from building the temple until the reign of Darius. Like Sheshbazzar, Zerubbabel disappears from Ezra-Nehemiah without explanation. That is, there is no mention of his death or his further activities following the completion of the temple.

Scholars have tended to assume that Sheshbazzar led a group of returnees in 538 that for unknown reasons failed and that Zerubbabel came some time between 538 and 520, presumably after Sheshbazzar's death, and eventually succeeded in completing the temple. The author of Ezra-Nehemiah has, to some extent, collapsed the two missions into one. More troubling is the fact that Ezra 5:16 ascribes to Sheshbazzar the laying of the foundation of the temple, while 3:8-13 attributes this to Zerubbabel. In addition, Neh 12:47 mentions Zerubbabel and Nehemiah together apparently as the beginning and end of the restoration. The discrepancy may be accounted for by the context of Ezra 5:16. It lies within a letter from a Persian official reporting the response of the Jews engaged in the temple reconstruction. The mention of Sheshbazzar as the founder of the temple, therefore, may reflect exaggeration on the part of the returnees who sought to emphasize the length of time that the temple reconstruction remained incomplete through no fault of their own, since they tried to carry out Cyrus's edict from the beginning.

Dates of Ezra and Nehemiah

As it stands, the book of Ezra-Nehemiah presents Ezra as having come to Jerusalem first in the seventh year of King Artaxerxes (Ezra 7:7-8) and Nehemiah after him in Artaxerxes's twentieth year (Neh 1:1; 2:1; 5:14). Nehemiah stayed in Jerusalem twelve years (Neh 5:14; 13:6) and then returned for a second visit some time during Artaxerxes's reign (13:6). Assuming that the Artaxerxes in all these verses is one and the same king, i.e., Artaxerxes I (465-424/423 B.C.E.), the date of Ezra's arrival would be 458, while Nehemiah arrived in 445. The two men are named together in Neh 8:9 on the occasion of Ezra's public reading of the law and in Neh 12:26 following the list of priests and Levites. Ezra is also mentioned in Neh 12:33, 36 among the leaders at the dedication of the wall led by Nehemiah. These three references, therefore, leave the impression that Ezra remained in Jerusalem until after Nehemiah's arrival in 445.

Nehemiah's dates have never been questioned and even receive substantiation from extrabiblical sources.[4] However, Ezra's dates have been debated among scholars since 1890, when a Belgian scholar named Albin

---

4. Papyri discovered on the Egyptian island of Elephantine indicate that by 407 B.C.E. Sanballat, the governor of Samaria who opposed Nehemiah (Neh 2:10, 19; 4:1, 7; 6:1, 2, 5, 12; 13:28), was an old man, whose sons were managing his affairs. See Bezalel Porten and Ada Yardeni, *Textbook of Aramaic Documents from Ancient Egypt*, vol. 1: *Letters* (Jerusalem: Hebrew University, 1986) 68-71.

van Hoonacker proposed reversing the order of Ezra-Nehemiah by identifying the Artaxerxes of Ezra 7:1, 7 as Artaxerxes II (405-359/358) rather than Artaxerxes I (465-424/423). Thus, the date of Ezra's arrival in Jerusalem would be 398 rather than 458.

There are several features of Ezra-Nehemiah that van Hoonacker and scholars since him have identified as problematic for the traditional Ezra-Nehemiah sequence and dates. First, aside from the verses noted above (Neh 8:9; 12:26, 33, 36), Ezra and Nehemiah are not mentioned together in the book; they do not work together or refer to one another, despite the fact that their missions are quite similar. Moreover, the three references to their interaction all appear to be secondary or artificial. The account of Ezra's reading of the law in Nehemiah 8–9, for instance, is part of Ezra's memoirs, as we have seen, and it seems unlikely that Ezra would have waited thirteen years to hold a public reading of the law, as indicated by the traditional chronology.

Second, the descriptions of conditions encountered by each of the reformers might indicate that Nehemiah preceded Ezra rather than the other way around. If Ezra's reforms, such as the prohibition of mixed marriage, had been implemented, why would Nehemiah have had to call for the same measures? The reference in Ezra 10:1 to a sizeable population in Jerusalem, while Nehemiah (7:4; 11:1-2) found it sparsely inhabited, has also been taken as evidence that the latter preceded the former, as has the mention of a wall in Ezra 9:9, when Nehemiah found Jerusalem in need of a city wall.

Finally, Ezra stayed in the chamber of Jehohanan son of Eliashib — presumably a room within the temple complex — according to Ezra 10:6. Yet Eliashib was the high priest in Nehemiah's day (Neh 3:1, 20-21; 13:4, 7, 28), and he had a grandson named Johanan (Neh 12:23). If they are the same individuals, then Ezra must have come after Nehemiah.

Of these three sets of arguments, the ones in the first set establish the distinctiveness of Ezra's and Nehemiah's missions but not Nehemiah's priority. It is indeed the case that Ezra and Nehemiah seem to have been on separate missions as their distinct memoirs indicate. Since Nehemiah 8–9 are widely recognized as belonging with Ezra's memoirs, their original location was earlier — probably directly after Ezra 8. Hence, there is no reason to assume that Ezra waited thirteen years to read the law. He may have done so shortly after his arrival to Jerusalem. The reference to Nehemiah in Neh 8:9 is almost certainly secondary. It does not appear in the parallel in

1 Esd 9:49, and his title "governor" is lacking in the LXX. The verb is singular, so that its original subject was apparently Ezra alone. In Neh 12:33, "Ezra" is a gloss identifying him with Azariah. The references to Ezra in 12:26, 36 seem to be afterthoughts. This is especially so in 12:36, where Ezra's name comes at the end of a list of priests whom he supposedly leads in procession. There is good reason, then, to believe that Ezra and Nehemiah conducted distinct missions, but there is nothing in this regard to call the traditional dates of 458 and 445 into question.

The arguments in the other two categories also weaken under scrutiny. The reforms introduced by Ezra may not have taken hold among the people, especially if his personal involvement was relatively brief, enduring only a year or so. Thirteen years would have passed between Ezra's arrival in 458 and Nehemiah's in 445, plenty of time for people to stray from Ezra's teachings, particularly if they had not been widely accepted or well grounded to begin with. Furthermore, it has been observed that Nehemiah appears to deal with abuses against an accepted way of life, which would presuppose Ezra's integration of Torah principles into the community life.[5] The differences between statements about the population of Jerusalem under Ezra and Nehemiah are overstated. Ezra 10:1 says that a very great assembly "from all Israel" gathered to Ezra in Jerusalem. It does not state that Jerusalem itself was heavily populated and so might accord with the statements in Neh 7:4; 11:1-2 indicating that there were few people settled in the city. There could also have been population shifts due to famine, disease, or the simple migration to agricultural settings during the thirteen years between the arrivals of Ezra and Nehemiah that would account for a difference in the city's population. The different statements about the wall are also overblown. The wall in Ezra 9:9 is "in Judea and Jerusalem" and should probably be understood metaphorically as protection rather than the literal wall around the city (Neh 7:1). In fact, the words for "wall" in these two verses are different.

As for the argument regarding J(eh)ohanan and Eliashib, both are common names and may not refer to the same individuals. This is especially so considering the fact that the relationship of the two in Ezra 10:6 and Neh 12:23 is not identical (son vs. grandson). Also, Ezra 10:6 does not state that this was the high priestly family, as is usually made explicit in Nehemiah. If it could be shown that the two texts referred to the same in-

5. Ralph W. Klein, "Ezra-Nehemiah, Books of," *ABD* 2:736.

dividuals, it would be a strong argument but not necessarily conclusive. The reference to the "chamber of Jehohanan son of Eliashib" might be the designation for the room in the author's day but not at the time of Ezra's visit.

In sum, there is compelling evidence for seeing the missions of Ezra and Nehemiah as distinct but not for reversing the order most naturally assigned to them on the basis of their presentation in the book — Ezra in the seventh year of Artaxerxes I (458) and Nehemiah in the twentieth year of the same king (445).[6]

Authorship and Date

Chapter Two above discussed in detail the relationship of Ezra-Nehemiah to Chronicles. To summarize, a long-standing consensus about the original unity of Chronicles-Ezra-Nehemiah began to dissipate in the 1960s and 1970s with new reconsiderations of the evidence for this viewpoint. As a result, there is a new consensus that most of the evidence is inconclusive but tends to favor regarding Chronicles and Ezra-Nehemiah as originally separate works based especially on theological and ideological differences between them.

The date of composition of Ezra-Nehemiah depends to a large extent on the date assigned to Ezra's arrival. If Ezra arrived in 458, then the earliest possible date for the book would be after Nehemiah's return visit during Artaxerxes I's reign, which ended in 424-423 B.C.E. If Ezra arrived in 398, then that becomes the earliest possible date of composition. In general, most scholars date the book some time in the period from 400-300 B.C.E., and it is hard to be more precise.

---

6. A third alternative would emend Ezra 7:7-8 to read that Ezra came to Jerusalem in the thirty-seventh year rather than the seventh of Artaxerxes (= 428 B.C.), thus placing Ezra and Nehemiah together during the latter's second visit to Jerusalem. See John Bright, *A History of Israel*, 3rd ed. (Philadelphia: Westminster, 1981) 400-401. This theory fails to explain why Ezra and Nehemiah have so little to do with each other directly. Also, its grounds for textual emendation are hypothetical without any versional or manuscript evidence. It has been roundly criticized and can boast few adherents at present. See John Emerton, "Did Ezra Go to Jerusalem in 428 B.C.?" *JTS* 17 (1966) 1-19. Emerton, though, subscribes to the 398 date.

Contents

Ezra 1–6

The book of Ezra-Nehemiah begins with the Cyrus edict (1:1-4). The author explains that Cyrus issued this edict because Yahweh aroused him to do so (v. 1). The financial assistance called for by the edict (v. 4) and rendered by the neighbors (v. 6) probably simply grants permission for Jewish colonies in Persia to support the returnees. Still, the support is reminiscent of the aid given to the Israelites by the Egyptians at the exodus (Exod 11:2-3; 12:35-36) and helps to cast the return theologically as a renewed exodus. King Cyrus also releases the temple vessels to Sheshbazzar for return (Ezra 1:8). The list in 1:9-10 may have been drawn from an inventory of these vessels. The list of returnees in Ezra 2 consists of three sections: laypersons, priests, and Levites. The list probably included names from different returns. In addition, this version of the list is probably dependent on the one in Nehemiah 7, although both ultimately derive from an older, independent document.[7]

In Ezra 3 Sheshbazzar has disappeared, and Zerubbabel and Jeshua are the leaders. They keep the Festival of Booths (Sukkot) and lay the foundation of the temple. It is not clear whether those who weep on this occasion (v. 12) do so out of disappointment from a comparison with the previous temple (cf. Hag 2:3) or out of nostalgia.[8] As noted earlier, the correspondence related in Ezra 4 comes from a later period and is out of place historically. However, its function is to illustrate the opposition from the "people of the land" that caused a delay in the construction efforts. Construction resumes at the urging of the prophets Haggai and Zechariah (5:1) and continues to completion as a result of the positive reply that the governor, Tattenai, receives from King Darius to his inquiry. This section of the book ends with an account of the celebration of Passover (6:19-22).

7. See the discussion of H. G. M. Williamson, *Ezra, Nehemiah*. WBC 16 (Waco: Word, 1985) 28-32.

8. As suggested by Nelson, *The Historical Books*, 170, n. 5.

Ezra 7–10

The narrative jumps over fifty-seven years to the reign of Artaxerxes (assuming this is Artaxerxes I) and the introduction of Ezra, who is designated a "scribe skilled in the law of Moses" (7:6) and a "scholar of the words of the commandments of Yahweh and his statutes over Israel" (7:11). The account is a mixture of third and first person narration, the latter sometimes known as Ezra's memoir. The authorization for Ezra's mission (7:11-26) is in Aramaic and purports to be a source document. Ezra 8 lists the family heads of those who accompanied Ezra as well as his preparations and his arrival in Jerusalem. Chapters 9–10 detail his handling of the crisis of mixed marriages and end with a list of those who put away their foreign wives and children.

Nehemiah 1–7

Nehemiah's memoir begins with a report that reaches him while he is serving as an official in the court of Artaxerxes in Susa. The report from his brother informs him of the sorry conditions of Jerusalem and its state of disrepair. The report elicits Nehemiah's prayer of confession and request for help (Neh 1:4-11). Nehemiah's distress at the report is noticed by King Artaxerxes, who sponsors his mission to rebuild Jerusalem's wall (2:1-8). Upon his arrival, Nehemiah undertakes an inspection of the city and calls for work to begin (2:11-18). The derision and opposition of Sanballat and those with him begins (2:9-10, 19-20). Chapter 3 lists the individuals who worked on different sections of the wall. The list does not mention Nehemiah and was probably not an original part of the Nehemiah memoir, though it may have been included in the memoir at a later stage.

The next three chapters describe three obstacles faced and overcome by Nehemiah and the workers. First, in ch. 4, are the intimidation and threats of attack leveled by Sanballat and company. These Nehemiah counters by encouragement to faith and by arming half of the workers and stationing them to stand guard while the other half works on the wall. In ch. 5, the obstacle is economic. The hardships caused by drought and concentration on the building of the wall are compounded by taxes and interest charged by the wealthier Jews, including Nehemiah (v. 10). Nehemiah persuades them to stop exacting interest (5:1-13). The second part of the chapter is later, as it reflects on Nehemiah's practice during his term as governor. However, it is related to the preceding in that Nehemiah claims that he provided generously for those who dined at his table without accepting the food allowance due the governor. Chapter 6 describes plots against Nehemiah himself through personal attack (vv. 1-4), accusation of rebellion (vv. 5-9), and intimidation that would have caused him to enter a part of the temple reserved only for priests (vv. 10-14). Despite these threats, the city wall is completed (vv. 15-19).

Chapter 7 moves from the completion of the wall to a notice about the sparseness of the city's population (v. 4), which in turn introduces the list of returnees that is essentially the same as that found in Ezra 2. Scholars debate whether the list was ever included in the Nehemiah memoir. The two versions of the list frame the account of the return in its various stages in response to Cyrus's edict. The version of the list in Nehemiah 7 also identifies the legitimate members of the postexilic community.

Nehemiah 8–13

The final section of the book consists of two main parts. Chapters 8–10 describe the religious climax to the rebuilding efforts with a reading of the law, confession, and a written affirmation of commitment to follow it. The reading of the law (8:1-12), at least, was once a part of Ezra's memoirs and probably originally followed directly after Ezra 8. There has been some discussion among scholars as to the identity of this law, the majority view holding that it was the Pentateuch in its present form or something close to it. Those who hear the law are motivated by it to keep the Festival of Booths (Sukkot), as recorded in the remainder of the chapter. They are further motivated to confession of sins (9:1-5). Then, urged by a recitation of Israel's history in the form of prayer in the rest of ch. 9, they commit to follow the law and submit to various obligations that they understand as deriving from this commitment (ch. 10). The list of names of the signatories in 9:38–10:27 comes almost entirely from previous lists and is probably artificial.

The second part of this section, chs. 11–13, begins with a list of those who were designated by lot to live in Jerusalem (11:1-20). A similar list in 1 Chr 9:2-17 refers to the first returnees from exile. The list in Neh 11:1-20 was supplemented by those named in vv. 21-36 and continuing in 12:1-26.

That is, the list of those living in Jerusalem in 11:1-20 originally was followed by the account of the dedication of the city wall in 12:27-43. The lists of priests and Levites in 12:1-26 are attributed to two different periods — the time of Jeshua and Zerubbabel (vv. 1-11) and the time of Joiakim, Jeshua's son (vv. 12-26). The list in 12:12-21 consists of twenty-two priestly houses, each with its head at the time of Joiakim. Thus, the first house is that of Seraiah, and its head is Meraiah (v. 12). Comparison of this list with the one in 12:1-7 indicates that the latter has been formed by taking the names of the priestly houses as individuals. The remainder of the chapter and continuing into ch. 13 (12:44–13:3) is an addition to the Nehemiah memoir designed to show that the measures undertaken by Nehemiah concerning separation from foreigners and tithing (13:4-13) were based on the law and traditional practice.

The rest of ch. 13 comes from Nehemiah's memoir and consists of three segments. The first in 13:4-14 describes corrections of abuses that Nehemiah makes on his return visit. In vv. 4-9, he evicts Tobiah from a room he has been using in the temple precincts. In vv. 10-14, Nehemiah restores the system of tithes and compensation for the Levites. The next two segments are each marked by the beginning formula "in those days" (vv. 15, 23). Verses 15-22 describe Nehemiah's correction of Sabbath abuses. Verses 23-29 relate another episode dealing with mixed marriages and, in this instance, children of such marriages who could not speak the language of Judah. One of the offenders is the grandson of the high priest who had married the daughter of Nehemiah's old enemy, Sanballat (vv. 28-29). The book of Ezra-Nehemiah ends in 13:30-31 with a kind of summary of Nehemiah's reforms in three categories: cleansing from everything foreign, establishing the duties of the cultic personnel, and providing for the continued tithes and offerings. This summary is drawn from Nehemiah's memoir and concludes with a plea for God to remember him for good.

Theological Themes

As important as Ezra-Nehemiah is as a historical source, it is also a significant theological document. In fact, its portrait of history has obviously been influenced by theological concerns. For convenience, I shall discuss the major themes of the book under the following three categories: Yahweh and history, identity and community, and the law.

Yahweh and History

The book begins by showing how Yahweh aroused the spirit of King Cyrus of Persia to release the exiles. Similar points are made throughout the book. At the end of the first section of Ezra (6:22), for instance, is a note that Yahweh turned the heart of the king of Assyria (= the king of Persia) to the exiles. Ezra's prayer (ch. 9) observes that God showed loving loyalty *(ḥesed)* to his people before the Persian kings. Then, Nehemiah's mission, like Ezra's, is supported by the Persian monarch. The book thus shows Yahweh to be in charge of human history. It is Yahweh who motivates the Persian kings to act on behalf of the Jews initially and then to support and protect them in their rebuilding efforts against their opponents. This portrayal of Yahweh stresses his faithfulness toward his people (Ezra 1:1) and elicits faithfulness and obedience toward him on their part. Nehemiah appeals to Yahweh's faithfulness in his requests, one of which ends the book, that Yahweh remember and reward him for the good he has done (Neh 13:31). Ezra 1:1 also makes clear that Yahweh honors and fulfills the words of his prophets, an observation that reinforces the urgings of Haggai and Zechariah toward completing the temple construction (Ezra 5:1).

Identity and Community

The most difficult aspect of Ezra-Nehemiah for modern readers is likely its repeated mandate for the returnees to separate themselves from foreigners, particularly the "people of the land," even to the point of demanding the divorce of foreign wives and dismissal of their children. This demand is in contrast to the much more charitable view of non-Israelites found in Chronicles. In Ezra-Nehemiah, however, it should be seen in the context of the returnees' search for a national and religious identity and community, to which mixed marriages are perceived as a threat. This quest for identity and community drives all phases of Ezra-Nehemiah — the rebuilding of the temple, Ezra's mission to consolidate the community, and Nehemiah's mission to build the wall around Jerusalem. The temple was the first order of business for the returnees (Ezra 1–6), for it served as the center of life for them. The proper maintenance of its rituals and the oversight and support of its personnel, therefore, were matters of the utmost importance. Then, the community had to be consolidated and purged of potentially corrupting influences. This was, in effect, Ezra's mission (Ezra 7–10 + Nehemiah 8–10). Finally, the sacred community needed to be isolated from the threat of foreigners. Hence, it was Nehemiah's task to build the walls around Jerusalem in order to ensure the safety of the community.

An important aspect of the search for identity, especially in relation to the "people of the land," concerns the issue of legitimacy. Who is the true Jew — the one who remained behind in the land or the one who has returned from exile? For Ezra-Nehemiah, the answer is obviously the latter. The claim for this group's legitimacy is based on several factors involving continuity with Israel's past (Nehemiah 9; 12:44-45) and adherence to the law. The temple vessels brought back by the returnees (Ezra 1:9-10) form continuity with the past as do the construction of the temple and its altar on their original sites (Ezra 3:3; 6:7). For individuals, membership in the community is supported by the lists of returnees as well as genealogies. Thus, persons claiming priestly status who are unable to demonstrate genealogical heritage are not allowed to serve (Ezra 2:62-63).

Perhaps as significant as what Ezra-Nehemiah says about the reconstructed community is what it does not say. There is no expression of hope in the restoration of the Davidic monarchy. No Davidic lineage is proffered for Sheshbazzar and Zerubbabel. Perhaps this is partly due to political expediency in the face of Persian rule. Ezra's recognition that the returnees remain slaves (Ezra 9:8-9) hints at a latent hope that they may some day be free of all bonds. However, at least in the meantime, the message seems to be that the restoration community can thrive under the Persians, especially in view of Yahweh's motivation of the Persian kings to allow its creation.

Law

Teaching the law was integral to Ezra's mission and was commanded in Artaxerxes's commission to him (Ezra 7:25). Ezra's public reading of the law (Neh 8:1-12) marked the climax of his mission, and in its present location this account is the climax of the book as a whole. Whatever the exact form of Ezra's law book, it was clearly the law of Moses. Hence, its instruction *(tôrāh)* and obedience were a part of the continuity of the postexilic community with preexilic Israel. Ezra required obedience to the law of all true Jews, making this a test or a sign of their identity and legitimacy as the true heirs of Israel. The reforms undertaken by Ezra and Nehemiah are based on the law. It is presented, therefore, as the foundation and guide for life in the community of true Israel — in short, Scripture. The reading of the law leads the returnees to contrition at the recognition that they have failed to follow it as they should. This failing is also in continuity with their forebears, as the rehearsal of Israel's history in the following chapter, Nehemiah 9, makes clear. Their contrition leads to confession and prayer for forgiveness (ch. 9), which is followed by a covenant and recommitment to keep the law and all of its commandments (ch. 10).

Bibliography

Arnold, Bill T., and H. G. M. Williamson. *Dictionary of the Old Testament: Historical Books.* Downers Grove: InterVarsity, 2005.

Baillet, M. "Textes des grottes 2Q, 3Q, 6Q, 7Q à 10Q." In *Les 'Petites Grottes' de Qumrân*, ed. Baillet, J. T. Milik, and R. de Vaux. *DJD* 3:45-164.

Barnes, William Hamilton. *Studies in the Chronology of the Divided Monarchy of Israel.* HSM 48. Atlanta: Scholars, 1991.

Barthélemy, Dominique. "1QJudg." In *Qumran Cave I*, ed. Barthélemy and J. T. Milik. *DJD* 1 (1955) 62-64.

Bodine, Walter Ray. *The Greek Text of Judges: Recensional Developments.* HSM 23. Chico: Scholars, 1980.

Bright, John. *A History of Israel.* 3rd ed. Philadelphia: Westminster, 1981.

Campbell, Antony F. *Of Prophets and Kings: A Late Ninth Century Document (1 Samuel 1–2 Kings 10).* CBQMS 17. Washington: Catholic Biblical Association, 1986.

————, and Mark A. O'Brien. *Unfolding the Deuteronomistic History: Origins, Upgrades, Present Text.* Minneapolis: Fortress, 2000.

Chisholm, Robert B., Jr. *Interpreting the Historical Books: An Exegetical Handbook.* Handbooks for Old Testament Exegesis. Grand Rapids: Kregel, 2006.

Crawford, Sidnie White. *Rewriting Scripture in Second Temple Times.* SDSSRL. Grand Rapids: Wm. B. Eerdmans, 2008.

Cross, Frank Moore, Jr. *Canaanite Myth and Hebrew Epic: Essays in the History of the Religion of Israel.* Cambridge: Harvard University Press, 1973.

————. "The Structure of the Deuteronomic History." In *Perspectives in Jewish Learning*, 9-24. Annual of the College of Jewish Studies 3. Chicago: Spertus College of Judaica, 1968.

Curtis, Adrian H. W. *Joshua*. OTG. Sheffield: Sheffield Academic, 1994.

Dietrich, Walter. *Prophetie und Geschichte: Eine redaktionsgeschichtliche Untersuchung zum deuteronomistischen Geschichtswerk*. FRLANT 108. Göttingen: Vandenhoeck & Ruprecht, 1972.

Emerton, John. "Did Ezra Go to Jerusalem in 428 B.C.?" *JTS* N.S. 17 (1966) 1-19.

Finkelstein, Israel, and Neil Asher Silberman. *The Bible Unearthed: Archaeology's New Vision of Ancient Israel and the Origin of Its Sacred Texts*. New York: Free Press, 2001.

————. *David and Solomon: In Search of the Bible's Sacred Kings and the Roots of the Western Tradition*. New York: Free Press, 2006.

Finley, Moses I. *Ancient History: Evidence and Models*. New York: Viking, 1986.

Galil, Gershon. *The Chronology of the Kings of Israel and Judah*. Studies in the History and Culture of the Ancient Near East 9. Leiden: Brill, 1996.

Halpern, Baruch. *The First Historians: The Hebrew Bible and History*. San Franciso: Harper & Row, 1988.

————, and David S. Vanderhooft. "The Editions of Kings in the 7th-6th Centuries B.C.E." *HUCA* 62 (1991) 179-244.

Hamilton, Victor P. *Handbook on the Historical Books*. Grand Rapids: Baker, 2001.

Hawk, L. Daniel. "Joshua, Book of." *DOTHB*, 563-75.

Holloway, Steven W. "Kings, Book of 1-2." *ABD* 4:69-83.

Japhet, Sara. "The Supposed Common Authorship of Chronicles and Ezra-Nehemiah Investigated Anew." *VT* 18 (1968) 330-71.

Kalimi, Isaac. *The Reshaping of Ancient Israelite History in Chronicles*. Winona Lake: Eisenbrauns, 2005.

van Keulen, Percy S. F. *Manasseh Through the Eyes of the Deuteronomists: The Manasseh Account (2 Kings 21:1-18) and the Final Chapters of the Deuteronomistic History*. OtSt 38. Leiden: Brill, 1996.

Klein, Ralph W. "Ezra and Nehemiah, Books of." *NIDB* 2:398-404.

————. "Ezra-Nehemiah, Books of." *ABD* 2:731-42.

————. *Textual Criticism of the Old Testament: The Septuagint after Qumran*. GBS. Philadelphia: Fortress, 1974.

Kuhrt, Amélie. "Persia, Persians." *DOTHB*, 768-82.

————. *The Persian Empire: A Corpus of Sources from the Achaemenid Period*. London: Routledge, 2007.

Lemke, Werner E. "The Synoptic Problem in the Chronicler's History." *HTR* 58 (1965) 349-63.

―――. "Synoptic Studies in the Chronicler's History." Diss., Harvard, 1963.

Long, V. Philips. *The Art of Biblical History.* Foundations of Contemporary Interpretation 5. Grand Rapids: Zondervan, 1994.

McCarter, P. Kyle. *Textual Criticism: Recovering the Text of the Hebrew Bible.* GBS. Philadelphia: Fortress, 1986.

McKenzie, Steven L. "The Chronicler as Redactor." In *The Chronicler as Author: Studies in Text and Texture,* ed. M. Patrick Graham and McKenzie, 70-90. JSOTSup 263. Sheffield: Sheffield Academic, 1999.

―――. "Historiography, Old Testament." *DOTHB,* 418-25.

―――. *How to Read the Bible: History, Prophecy, Literature — Why Modern Readers Need to Know the Difference and What It Means for Faith Today.* New York: Oxford University Press, 2005.

―――. "The So-Called Succession Narrative in the Deuteronomistic History." In *Die sogenannte Thronfolgegeschichte Davids: Neue Einsichten und Anfragen,* ed. Albert de Pury and Thomas Römer, 123-35. OBO 176. Freiburg: Universitätsverlag, 2000.

―――. *The Trouble with Kings: The Composition of the Book of Kings in the Deuteronomistic History.* VTSup 42. Leiden: Brill, 1991.

―――, and Stephen R. Haynes, eds. *To Each Its Own Meaning: An Introduction to Biblical Criticisms and Their Application.* 2nd ed. Louisville: Westminster John Knox, 1999.

Milik, J. T. "Textes de la grotte 5Q." In *Les 'Petites Grottes' de Qumrân,* ed. M. Baillet, Milik, and R. de Vaux. *DJD* 3 (1962) 165-97.

Miller, J. Maxwell. "The Omride Dynasty in the Light of Recent Literary and Archaeological Research." Diss., Emory, 1964.

Nelson, Richard D. *The Double Redaction of the Deuteronomistic History.* JSOTSup 18. Sheffield: JSOT, 1981.

―――. *The Historical Books.* Interpreting Biblical Texts. Nashville: Abingdon, 1998.

―――. *Joshua.* OTL. Louisville: Westminster John Knox, 1997.

Noth, Martin. *The Deuteronomistic History.* JSOTSup 15. 2nd ed. Sheffield: JSOT, 1991.

Petersen, David L. *Late Israelite Prophecy: Studies in Deutero-Prophetic Literature and in Chronicles.* SBLMS 23. Missoula: Scholars, 1977.

Porten, Bezalel, and Ada Yardeni. *Textbook of Aramaic Documents from Egypt.* Vol. 1: *Letters.* Jerusalem: Hebrew University, 1986.

Provan, Iain W. *Hezekiah and the Book of Kings: A Contribution to the Debate about the Composition of the Deuteronomistic History.* BZAW 172. Berlin: de Gruyter, 1988.

von Rad, Gerhard. "The Beginnings of Historical Writing in Ancient Israel." In *The Problem of the Hexateuch and Other Essays,* 166-204. New York: McGraw-Hill, 1966.

————. "Die deuteronomistische Geschichtstheologie in den Königsbüchern." In *Deuteronomium Studien,* B, 52-64. FRLANT N.S. 40. Göttingen: Vandenhoeck & Ruprecht, 1947 = "The Deuteronomistic Theology of History in the Books of Kings." In *Studies in Deuteronomy,* 74-91. SBT 9. Chicago: Regnery, 1953.

Römer, Thomas. *The So-Called Deuteronomistic History: A Sociological, Historical, and Literary Introduction.* London: T&T Clark, 2005.

————, and Albert de Pury. "Deuteronomistic Historiography (DH): History of Research and Debated Issues." In *Israel Constructs Its History: Deuteronomistic Historiography in Recent Research,* ed. de Pury, Römer, and Jean-Daniel. Macchi, 24-141. JSOTSup 306. Sheffield: Sheffield Academic, 2000.

Rost, Leonhard. *Die Überlieferung von der Thronnachfolge Davids.* BWANT 3/6. Stuttgart: Kohlhammer, 1926 = *The Succession to the Throne of David.* Historic Texts and Interpreters in Biblical Scholarship. Sheffield: Almond, 1982.

Shenkel, James Donald. *Chronology and Recensional Development in the Greek Text of Kings.* HSM 1. Cambridge, MA: Harvard University Press, 1968.

Smend, Rudolf. "Das Gesetz und die Völker: Ein Beitrag zur deuteronomistischen Redaktionsgeschichte." In *Probleme biblischer Theologie. Gerhard von Rad zum 70. Geburtstag,* ed. Hans Walter Wolff, 494-509. Munich: Kaiser, 1971.

Talmon, Shemaryahu. "Ezra and Nehemiah (Books and Men)." *IDBSup,* 317-28.

Tetley, M. Christine. *The Reconstructed Chronology of the Divided Kingdom.* Winona Lake: Eisenbrauns, 2005.

Thiele, Edwin R. *The Mysterious Numbers of the Hebrew Kings: A Reconstruction of the Chronology of the Kingdoms of Israel and Judah.* Chicago: University of Chicago Press, 1951.

Tov, Emanuel. "4QJosh[b]." In *Qumran Cave 4.IX,* ed. Eugene C. Ulrich, Frank Moore Cross, et al. *DJD* 14 (1995) 153-60.

Trebolle Barrera, Julio. "4QJudg[a]." In *Qumran Cave 4.IX,* ed. Eugene C. Ulrich, Frank Moore Cross, et al. *DJD* 14 (1995) 161-64.

————. "4QJudg^b." In *Qumran Cave 4.IX*, ed. Eugene C. Ulrich, Frank Moore Cross, et al. *DJD* 14 (1995) 165-69.

————. "4QKgs." In *Qumran Cave 4.IX*, ed. Eugene C. Ulrich, Frank Moore Cross, et al. *DJD* 14 (1995) 171-83.

Ulrich, Eugene. *The Dead Sea Scrolls and the Origins of the Bible.* SDSSRL. Grand Rapids: Wm. B. Eerdmans, 1999.

————. "4QJosh^a." In *Qumran Cave 4.IX*, ed. Ulrich, Frank Moore Cross, et al. *DJD* 14 (1995) 143-52.

Van Seters, John. *The Biblical Saga of King David.* Winona Lake: Eisenbrauns, 2009.

————. "The Court History and DtrH." In *Die sogenannte Thronfolgegeschichte Davids: Neue Einsichten und Anfragen,* ed. Albert de Pury and Thomas Römer, 70-93. OBO 176. Freiburg: Universitätsverlag, 2000.

————. *In Search of History: Historiography in the Ancient World and the Origins of Biblical History.* New Haven: Yale University Press, 1983.

Veijola, Timo. *Die ewige Dynastie: David und die Entstehung seiner Dynastie nach der deuteronomistischen Darstellung.* AASF B 193. Helsinki: Suomalainen Tiedeakatemia, 1975.

————. *Das Königtum in der Beurteilung der deuteronomistischen Historiographie.* AASF B 198. Helsinki: Suomalainen Tiedeakatemia, 1977.

Weippert, Helga. "Die 'deuteronomistischen' Beurteilung der Könige von Israel und Juda und das Problem der Redaktion der Königsbücher." *Bib* 53 (1972) 301-39.

Williamson, H. G. M. *Ezra, Nehemiah.* WBC 16. Waco: Word, 1985.

————. *Israel in the Books of Chronicles.* Cambridge: Cambridge University Press, 1977.

Wilson, Robert R. *Genealogy and History in the Biblical World.* Yale Near Eastern Researches 7. New Haven: Yale University Press, 1977.

Wolff, Hans Walter. "Das Kerygma des deuteronomistischen Geschichtswerk." *ZAW* 73 (1961) 171-86 = "The Kerygma of the Deuteronomic Historical Work." In *The Vitality of Old Testament Traditions,* ed. Walter Brueggemann and Wolff, 83-100. 2nd ed. Atlanta: John Knox, 1982.

Zunz, Leopold. *Die gottesdienstlichen Vorträge der Juden.* Berlin: Asher, 1832.

Index of Names and Subjects

Index of Names and Subjects